AIR VANGUARD 13

ALBATROS D.III
Johannisthal, OAW, and Oeffag variants

JAMES F. MILLER

First published in Great Britain in 2014 by Osprey Publishing,
PO Box 883, Oxford, OX1 9PL, UK
PO Box 3985, New York, NY 10185-3985, USA
E-mail: info@ospreypublishing.com

Osprey Publishing is part of the Osprey Group

A CIP catalog record for this book is available from the British Library

Print ISBN: 978 1 78200 371 7
PDF ebook ISBN: 978 1 4728 0792 2
ePub ebook ISBN: 978 1 4728 0793 9

Index by Marie-Pierre Evans
Typeset in Deca Sans and Sabon
Originated by PDQ Media, Bungay, UK
Printed in China through Asia Pacific Offset Limited

14 15 16 17 18   10 9 8 7 6 5 4 3 2 1

Osprey Publishing is supporting the Woodland Trust, the UK's leading
woodland conservation charity, by funding the dedication of trees.

www.ospreypublishing.com

ACKNOWLEDGMENTS

The author wishes to thank the following for their selfless contributions:

Jim, Major, and LaFonda Miller; Lance Bronnenkant; Chris and Charyn
Cordry; Tom and Karen Dillon; Jon Guttman; Jack Herris; Bert Hughlett;
Reinhard Kastner; Peter Kilduff; Herb and Sarah Kilmer; League of
World War One Historians; Detlev Mahlo; Koloman Mayrhofer; James G.
and Judy Miller; Marton Szigeti; Greg VanWyngarden; Aaron Weaver;
Reinhard Zankl.

CONTENTS

ALBATROS D.III

Johannisthal, OAW, and Oeffag variants

INTRODUCTION

It is without question that mankind possesses an inexorable and inexhaustible need for knowledge and improvement. Because of this, today's technological innovation becomes tomorrow's antiquity. During war it is no different, although the high political and life-or-death stakes of war raise the bar and increase the rapidity of these advancements.

And so it was for the World War I fighter airplane. Unknown and undeveloped when the war began, necessity soon begot the creation of armed pusher airplanes that could use forward-firing weapons without risk of damaging a spinning propeller, since the engine and propeller were behind the pilot. Yet the pusher design was inherently draggy compared with the preferred tractor-powered designs – but how to overcome the spinning propeller? Resourcefulness often precedes technological advancement, and so it was that the French overcame propeller obstruction by mounting machine guns to the upper wing that fired *above* the propeller arc. This would suffice until technology caught up.

Meanwhile, both France and Germany had been developing mechanical means to use a tractor airplane to fire a machine gun through a spinning propeller arc. The Germans were the first to successfully incorporate it into a tractor-powered airplane design, the Fokker E-type monoplanes. Initially they were the only ones able to do so and this caused a period of concern known as "the Fokker Scourge," when their impact was felt against Entente reconnaissance two-seaters. Despite the success there was an increasing desire to improve the aerodynamic performance of the fighter and the number of guns it could carry; one machine gun was felt to be lacking and would leave the airplane unarmed if it jammed. The rotary engines of Fokker's monoplanes could not support the weight of two machine guns and associated ammunition; however, when larger rotary engines were used to bear that weight they exacted intolerable penalties against airplane performance.

The solution arrived via the Albatros company, makers of successful B- and C-type two-seater airplanes. Taking a 160Ps engine from one of their C-types, they installed it into a single-seat biplane fighter of new design. The result was a new machine with power enough to bear the weight of twin machine-gun armament yet still provide good speed, rate of climb, and acceptable maneuverability. Named the Albatros D.I, the type entered service in September 1916. The Royal Flying Corps (RFC) immediately took notice.

Unlike the vast schedules during peace that allowed time for adequate testing, the war dictated constant and expedient development and improvement. Even though the D.I had just entered service, Albatros had already designed and tested its eventual replacement, the D.II. Several new features were implemented but largely it was the same design. However, a third design, the D.III, employed redesigned wings that improved downward visibility for airplanes flown with the intention of stalking two-seater recon machines from above and then diving for the attack.

The rapidity of these advancements fostered a truncated period of testing and refinement, which had serious and tragic implications in the case of the D.III. A problem was discovered with the lower wings, in which an unknown design flaw could result in airframe deformation or the complete loss of structural integrity, often causing the death of the pilot. The exigencies of expediency dictated a largely in-field repair, and wing redesign also helped reduce future risk with machines still being produced – still, the risk never left entirely. Fortunately, later D.IIIs built by the Ostdeutsche Albatros Werke (OAW) and Austrian company Oesterreichische Flugzeugfabrik Allgemeine Gesellschaft (Oeffag) were built much more solidly, so the design evolution worked beyond the problem while satisfying the pressing urgency to "one-up" the enemy with technological advancement and innovation. This culminated with Oeffag's final D.III production type, the Series 253. With its solid construction and employment of the largest engine used on the type, it was the best Albatros D.III of the war.

Yet one expects improvement with innovation; otherwise, why innovate? Unfortunately, in this regard the German Albatros D.III fell short. By the time of its front-line arrival in very late December 1916 it was the third new Albatros D-type in as many months – but it brought no considerable new advantage, other than improved downward visibility. Worse, the Germans were saddled with the new design's fatal structural flaws. Mostly they overcame these obstacles; but when the RFC employed new designs with improved performance throughout 1917, and the D.III's successor the D.V neither improved performance nor eliminated the structural shortcomings of the lower wings, pilot morale for the Albatros began to wane. During the spring, however, despite its shortcomings, German pilots had flown the Albatros D.III with incredible success. It became the make and model with which many of Germany's most famous aces would attain a majority of their victories, and today it is regarded as one of Germany's most iconic fighters.

A mixture of Kest 1b Albatros D.III and D.III(OAW) machines. At casual glance the different models can be overlooked, or the D.III(OAW) confused with the Albatros D.V, due to their similar rudder shapes, but all have the D.III's classic slab-sided fuselages.

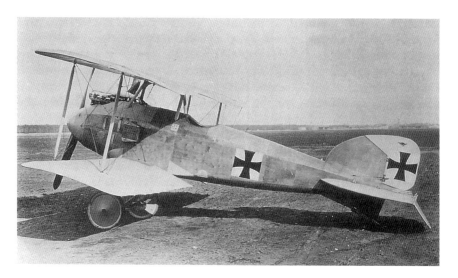

Albatros D.I prototype at Johannisthal. Note the clear doped linen wings, tail, and no windshield. Features changed prior to production include the upturned exhaust manifold, unbalanced elevator, externally routed rudder cables, and *Eisernes Kreuz* located on the rudder only. Wing root fairings are metal, although later they were often made of wood.

Fokker demonstrated his interrupter gear at Doberitz a month after the capture of Garros' airplane and was awarded a production contract for airplanes so equipped. As German Fliegertruppe Commander General Ernst von Hoeppner wrote in his postwar memoirs:

> The true *Kampfflugzeug* [combat airplane] originated first with the utilization of the invention of Fokker, which made it possible to fire through the propeller arc. The fixed machine-gun was now operated by the pilot himself. The omission of the observer produced in this new E-type plane extraordinary speed, maneuverability and climbing ability…

This new E-type was the Fokker E.I, a mid-wing monoplane powered by an air-cooled 80Ps rotary engine (*Pferdestärke*, or Ps, is a measure of horsepower, where 1.0hp equals 1.014Ps). By mid-1915 German pilots used this new weapon to attack enemy reconnaissance airplanes and this led to a desperate period for the Allies during which Germany held tactical air superiority. Initially the Allies had no effective machine with which to counter this threat and necessarily changed their tactics to state that "a machine proceeding on reconnaissance must be escorted by at least three other fighting machines … and a reconnaissance should not be continued if any machines become detached." Four airplanes were now required to do the work of one.

Meanwhile, as the battle of Verdun trudged through 1916 (nearly a year long, with almost one million casualties), the French urged a British offensive to lessen France's military burden. Toward that end, the British launched the Battle of the Somme on July 1. But by then "the Fokker Scourge" had been countered by the arrival of Allied single-seat biplane fighters, namely French Nieuports, and as the British and German armies slogged through yet another bloodbath – British casualties on the first day of the Battle of the Somme alone were some 19,000 killed and 41,000 wounded – British F.E.2 and DH.2 biplane pushers joined the French Nieuport in dominating the skies, enjoying complete superiority that they maintained throughout the summer.

Fokker attempted to alter this situation by increasing the power of his monoplanes with twin-row rotary engines and augmenting firepower with two and sometimes three machine guns (as seen with the Fokker E.IV), but these changes hamstrung performance to the point of pilot dissatisfaction. "In a climb," reported Germany's leading ace and Orden Pour le Mérite-decorated

Hauptmann Oswald Boelcke, "[the E.IV] loses speed to such an extent that Nieuport biplanes have repeatedly escaped me." This helped foster a sea change amongst the Fliegertruppe that future German machines ought to be of biplane rather than monoplane construction. Future 44-victory ace and Orden Pour le Mérite winner Obltn Rudolf Berthold opined, "we had fallen asleep on the laurel wreaths that the single-seaters in the hands of a few superlative pilots [Boelcke, Immelmann, Wintgens] had achieved. It was not the monoplane itself, but the pilots who were responsible for the success."

In early 1916 the airplane manufactures Halberstadt and Fokker began designing single-seat fighters that utilized in-line water-cooled engines, rather than the air-cooled rotary engines that powered the Fokker E-types. In March Halberstadt received a letter of intent authorizing the construction of 12 of their D.Is and D.IIs; the low production figure suggests Idflieg's caution with the company's inexperience. The letter specified these machines carry a 150kg (330lb) useful load that included one synchronized machine gun with 500 rounds of ammunition; a maximum speed of 145km/h (90mph); and the ability to climb to 4,000m (13,124 feet) in 40 minutes (an average of 100 meters per minute, or 325 feet per minute). These requirements were exceeded when the first production airplanes were flown in May.

Fokker, possessing deeper experience with single-seater types, albeit of monoplane configuration, was awarded an 80-machine contract for his single-seat biplane fighter, the Fokker D.I. The Fokker D.I began life in June 1916 as prototype M.18, a single-bay single-seater with the wing gap filled by the fuselage in the same manner as the LFG Roland C.II "Walfisch." The machine was powered by an in-line, water-cooled, 100Ps Mercedes D.I engine. Using a water-cooled engine was radically different than his usual use of rotary engines; Fokker claimed "the adaptation of the water-cooled engine for use in fighting planes by air headquarters came about through my efforts." Unfortunately, climb performance did not meet expectations, and by March the prototype had undergone several alterations.

In June, the 120Ps Halberstadt D.II was the first German biplane single-seat fighter to reach the front. Its superior qualities over the monoplane were noted in an Idflieg report in July: "The Halberstadt with the 120Ps Mercedes engine has flown at the Front with good results and is well regarded; especially praised are its ability to climb and maneouvre. It is decidedly preferred to the 160Ps [rotary engine] Fokker [E.IV]. However, everyone urgently requests twin machine guns but this will lead to a corresponding reduction in performance."

June was also the month that Albatros Flugzeugwerke GmbH – known theretofore solely for the production of two-seater machines during the war – was awarded a contract for 12 single-seater biplane fighters. Albatros's history harkens back to the development of German aviation, when during much of the first decade of the 20th century Germany's aviation aspirations focused on lighter- rather than heavier-than-air flight. Having formed a Luftschiffer Detachement (Lighter-than-air Detail) in 1884 to evaluate the reconnaissance applications of balloons, by 1901 the Detachement had grown into a Luftschiffer Batallion (Lighter-than-air Battalion) that employed free and moored balloons. In 1900 the first practical powered flight of a lighter-than-air machine occurred via a 17-minute flight of Graf Zeppelin's rigid airship LZ.1, and this event piqued the Kriegsministerium's (War Ministry's) interest in the craft's possible military usefulness. Still, new heavier-than-air machines were not unknown. In 1905 the Americans Orville and Wilbur Wright, from Ohio, brought their airplane to Europe to demonstrate controlled powered flight and illustrated its practicality via a flight of 39km. Yet the War Ministry conference of 1906 established that German military aeronautics ought to focus on rigid airships, in large part due to their familiarity with lighter-than-air machines versus the newer heavier-than-air machines.

The year 1909 saw an increase in the interest and development of the airplane. Public money was used to promote airplane development, demonstration flights were conducted, and the first German flight-meeting took place at the inaugural German aerodrome at Johannisthal, near Berlin. Various manufacturers came to Johannisthal and under license began building airplanes of foreign design, but in October a 3km flight at Johannisthal netted the pilot a 40,000 mark prize for the first flight of a German airplane powered by a German aero-engine. Lighter-than-air machines still remained the focus of the German military, but many people realized that the airplane was coming of age.

One such person was German biologist Dr Walther Huth. Born in Altenburg in1875, Huth was the son of a Prussian major and for 13 years had followed his family's traditional military career before leaving the service in 1908 to study natural sciences. After meeting French aviation pioneer Hubert Latham, Huth so embraced the thought of flight via airplane that he sent his chauffeur Simon Brunnhuber to France and paid for his flight training there. Upon its successful completion, Brunnhuber returned with a Levasseur Antoinette single-seat monoplane that Huth had purchased; later he also bought a Farman two-seater. With foresight enough to recognize the airplane's future importance toward military applications, Huth contacted the Kriegsministerium in October 1909 and offered the services of his airplanes for flight instruction, gratis, with Brunnhuber serving as

Jasta 16b LVG-built Albatros D.II (serial no. u/k), flown by Ltn Robert Dycke. The main difference from the D.I is the reduced wing gap and outwardly splayed N struts. Typical of LVG builds, the vertical stabilizer contains no serial number and a triangular company logo is affixed to the rudder, adjacent the bottom hinge.

instructor. While the subsequent negotiations were underway, Huth established his own company at Johannisthal that December, the Albatros Flugzeugwerke GmbH, named after the seabird with which he was familiar from his scientific studies.

Negotiations with the Militärbehörde (Military Authority) lasted until March 1910, when they accepted Huth's proposal. It is believed flight instruction began that July, and by March 1911 Brunnhuber had trained six pilots. Progress had been slow due to lack of funds, suitable training space (airplane engines frightened the horses of troops training nearby), and lingering doubts regarding the airplane's useful military role; there were also concerns about long training times for airplane maintenance personnel. Regardless, training continued as Albatros was contracted to build lattice-framed Farman reproductions with the type designation Albatros MZ.2.

In 1912 Albatros hired Diplom-Ingenieur (Engineering Graduate) Robert Thelen as chief designer. Born in Nürnberg on March 23, 1884, Thelen had studied mechanical engineering at the Royal Technical College of Charlottenburg in Berlin, graduating in 1909. A year later Thelen was the ninth German pilot trained (FAI [Fédération Aeronautique Internationale]-Brevet 9, from May 11, 1910) and became a competition pilot flying Wright biplanes. Teaming up with Diplom Ingenieur Helmut Hirth (FAI-Brevet 79 from March 11, 1911) and employing the perfected semi-monocoque wooden fuselage designs of Ober-Ingenieur Hugo Grohmann (a construction technique which provided enough strength via the external skin to eliminate the need for internal bracing, thereby reducing weight and increasing performance and payload capacity), Thelen's designs moved away from the Farman-type open-lattice construction as Albatros began building newly designed airplanes with the type of enclosed wooden fuselages for which they would become renowned (*Rumpf-Doppeldecker*, or fuselage double-decker [biplane]). Chief among these would be the Albatros Type DD, later known as the B.I, designed in early 1913 by Ernst Heinkel (whose future company produced many airplanes in World War II) and improved by Thelen's suggestions based on his experience as a pilot; Thelen referred to the type as "Albatros DD, system Heinkel-Thelen." Powered by a 100Ps Mercedes D.I engine, the semi-monocoque three-bay (*Dreistielig*) DD was a successful design that set several world records for duration and altitude in the months prior to World War I. That summer a single-bay version known as the *Renndoppeldecker* was powered by a 100Ps Hiero engine and won the

Unarmed Albatros D.III prototype at Johannisthal. Its sleek and ruggedly attractive lines belied structural problems with its new sesquiplane wing design, which featured the classic "V" interplane strut.

100km speed prize at the Aspern *Flugmeeting* in Vienna, Austria. Experience gained with this machine is considered to have sown the seeds for the future Albatros D.I.

After World War I broke fully in August 1914, Albatros concentrated on manufacturing two-seat B- and C- type machines. Aerial observation and artillery spotting were crucial for the support of ground forces and required that these machine types had manufacturing and engine allocation priority. As the war progressed the opposing forces developed single-seat fighters to protect their two-seater observation machines and destroy those of the enemy, but mostly these fighters had been powered by rotary engines; those powered by in-line engines had been somewhat hamstrung by a production lack of available higher horsepower engines, which were prioritized for the B- and C-type machines. This affected the early Fokker and Halberstadt D-types that employed 100 or 120Ps engines rather than those of 160Ps, although Fokker later claimed to be a victim of a conspiracy to deny him use of a 160Ps engine. In any event, engine availability did not lessen the born-from-experience calls from fighter pilots requesting single-engine machines be equipped with higher horsepower engines and armed with two rather than the then-standard single machine gun. Thoughts also surfaced among German pilots that while rotary engine fighters – with their rapid capacity for engine start and takeoff – were ideal for intercepting enemy machines, a fighter powered by the more reliable in-line engine and armed with twin machine guns would be suited to protect two-seater airplanes beyond the enemy lines. Although German aerial tactics evolved differently, this mindset came at a time of increasing engine manufacture productivity and set the stage for the birth of a new breed of fighter.

And none too soon. Tactical German aerial domination, which had once held sway with rotary-engined Fokker and Pfalz E-type wing-warping monoplanes, had been lost to the more nimble French Nieuport and British DH.2s that not only out-flew the German fighters but were available in greater numbers. Rather than compete with the maneuverability of these adversaries, the Thelen-led Albatros design bureau set to work on what became the Albatros D.I and D.II. By April 1916, they had developed a sleek yet rugged machine that featured the usual Albatros semi-monocoque wooden construction and employed a 160Ps Mercedes D.III engine. Visual hallmarks

ALBATROS D.III 643/17 OF OBLT ROBERT GREIM, JAGDSTAFFEL 34B, SUMMER 1917

Aside from dark-colored discs (depicted here as red) adorning the fuselage as personal markings, this late-production 600-series Johannisthal-built machine remained in factory condition. A photograph of this aircraft clearly shows the wings still featured Albatros's usual three-colored camouflage months after Idflieg's April directive to discontinue use of Venetian red. This directive has been interpreted to mean all 600 and 750-series Albatros D.IIIs used light and dark green only thereafter. However, the directive was issued to aircraft manufacturers two months *after* the 600-series Albatros D IIIs were even ordered – begging the question of why Albatros would discontinue use of Venetian red months before being ordered to do so – and said nothing about painting the wings light and dark green. It actually stated the wings were to be painted "dark green and lilac only," but by the time of its issuance most or nearly all of the Johannisthal-manufactured Albatrosses had already been built. There *may* have been some crossover with the final few machines of the last Johannisthal D.III 750-series production run, but photographs show dark green and lilac (commonly referred to as "mauve") made their debuts on OAW-built Albatros D.IIIs and Johannisthal-built Albatros D.Vs, both of which were ordered into production that April, the same month as the directive.

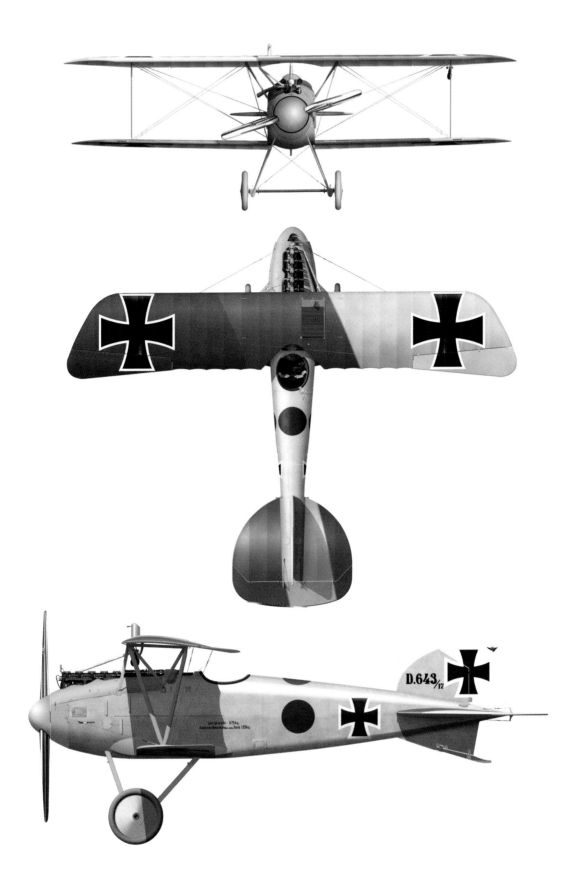

while "static tests and series production are being accelerated." At some point the wing load factors must have been determined to be satisfactory because in June, Idflieg initiated a production order for 400 D.IIIs, 1910–2309/16.

These airplanes began arriving in-field late December 1916 and were greeted by enthusiastic Jagdstaffel pilots who found the new machine was faster and climbed better than the barely months-old D.II. Experience with the new model soon revealed that gun-muzzle blast and particle discharge caused engine damage, necessitating metal tubes and blast panels be installed above the intake and exhaust manifolds, and the undercarriage and tailskid required strengthening. Furthermore, pilots complained that external coolant plumbing to and from the central wing radiator hampered aiming, and eventually the radiator was offset to starboard somewhere between machines 2215/16 and 2252/16. Often the reason for this relocation is attributed to pilots being scalded after radiator combat damage, but only the Albatros D-types had radiators so offset – that is, airplanes where forward vision for aiming was paramount. The Albatros C.X and C.XII were produced after the D.III but retained their centrally located radiators. Being the object of fighter attacks their radiators were just as susceptible to combat damage, and their pilots' lower faces – the only part of their bodies actually exposed to any scalding water, presuming they weren't wrapped in heavy scarves – were just as susceptible to burns as the faces of single-seater pilots. Moreover, Albatros's later prototype D-series fighters, such as the D.VII, D.IX, and D.X, retained centrally located radiators – but routed the external, vision-impeding plumbing well clear of the pilot's aiming line-of-sight. Offset radiators were not enough to prevent any leaking water from reaching the cockpit anyway, as modern Albatros reproduction pilots have revealed, and in any event bigger radiator problems arose with warmer spring weather when D.III radiators, 25 percent smaller than those of the D.II, began boiling over. Fortunately, in-field installation of a larger D.II radiator solved the problem and led to the installation of Daimler radiators in June.

However, the most noteworthy and now infamous teething trouble of the D.III involved its new sesquiplane configuration, specifically with the single-spar lower wings. Reports surfaced within weeks of the type's arrival that four D.IIIs had endured fractured ribs and broken leading edges resulting from dives and turning maneuvers. Albatros began supplying reinforcing braces and replacement wings to the afflicted airplanes, but on January 27 the D.IIIs were grounded due to continued wing failures spreading throughout the Staffeln.

ALBATROS D.III (OAW) OF HPTM FRANZ WALZ, FL ABT 304B, SUMMER 1918
Void of personal markings, this Albatros D.III (OAW) featured a factory-finished wooden fuselage, clear-doped rudder, and dark green and lilac wings and tail, the latter of which featured a span-wise color demarcation. Standard with OAW builds, upper wing crosses were centered on the aileron control arms, lower wing crosses were well outboard, and fuselage crosses were located nearly at midpoint between the cockpit and tail. Based in Palestine, this machine employed twin radiators to help improve engine cooling in the hot Middle East climate, where during summer the daytime ground temperatures could reach 35°C (95°F). Pilot Franz Walz had previously flown two-seaters with Kasta 2 of KG1, where he scored six victories, but when flying single-seaters in command of Jagdstaffeln 19 and 2 he attained not a single victory. In May 1917 legendary ace Werner Voss lobbied to have Walz replaced as Jasta 2 Staffelführer on the grounds of war-weariness and being unfit for command, resulting in a reprimand for Voss and Walz's request for transfer. This was granted. After less than two weeks with Jasta 34, Walz was sent to command Fl Abt 304b in Palestine, and in this capacity he performed such sterling service as to earn the Pour le Merite in August 1918.

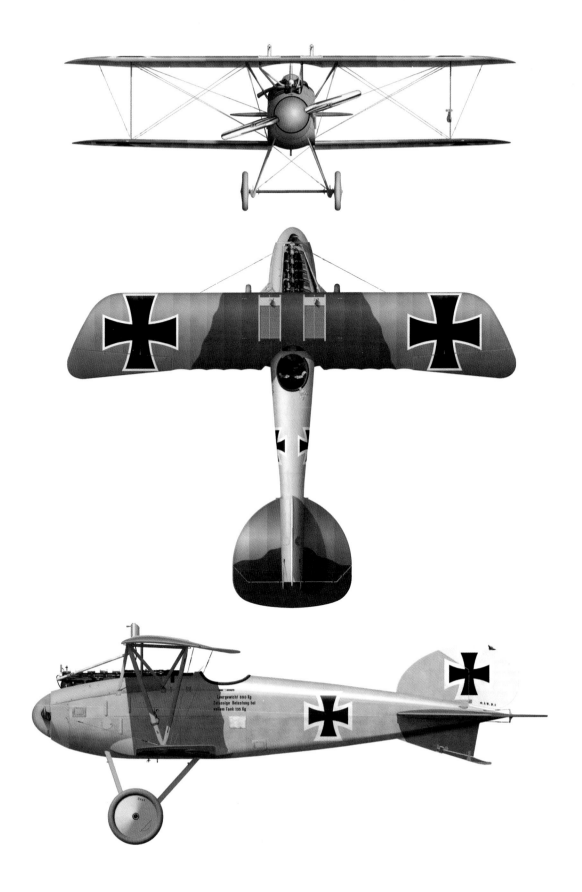

Several reinforced wings were designed, known as Wings 2–5 (Wing 1 was the originally manufactured wing), which employed wider rib webs, flanges, and magnolia veneer reinforcements; these wings were to be installed at the factory. Wing 5 was the same as Wing 1 but fitted with two (later three) 1.5mm sheet-steel reinforcement arms between the main spar and front stringer, to be installed in-field. Wings 2–5 were tested to satisfaction and the grounding was rescinded on February 19, although D.III losses prior to that date suggest the initial grounding order applied only to machines whose wings had not yet been reinforced. Still, although perhaps slowed, wing failures persisted despite these reinforcements, with ribs failing ahead of the spar and causing the leading edge to fold upward, after which the slipstream de-gloved the wing fabric. Further load tests could find no strength deficiencies in the modified wings and engineers could ascertain no finite cause for the problem, although they theorized vibration or unknown pressure distributions. A suspected contributing factor is divergence phenomena (wing twisting, or "flutter"), as inspections revealed the lower wing interplane V-strut attachment bolt holds had widened to allow the entire wing to become loose and rotate 2cm about the spar.

Overall, 508 Albatros D.IIIs were built at Johannisthal in three production batches: 400 machines, D.1910–2309/16, ordered October 1916; 50 machines, 600–649/17, ordered February 1917; and 50 machines, D.750–799/17, ordered March 1917. Along with these 500 airplanes Albatros also built three prototypes and five machines to test "basket weave" construction, whereby interwoven strips were sewn together and then sewn onto an airframe. Load tests after a three-week exposure to weather resulted in structural failure well below requirements, and after internal strengthening via longerons resulted in the same weight as production fuselages, the idea was abandoned.

Meanwhile, with the Albatros D-type design in a state of perpetual flux, construction of further D.IIIs shifted from Johannisthal to the OAW in Schneidemühl, enabling Albatros to construct the next D-type model, the D.V. OAW's first 200-machine D.III production order was penned April 23, 1917, D.1650–1849/17, the first two machines arriving for testing in June. No structural problems were encountered with the wings but the fuselage underwent strengthening after it failed at 73 percent of the required load. This and sundry other minor teething troubles were rectified and the D.III(OAW)

Albatros D.III(OAW) in Palestine. As the 600- and 750-series Johannisthal-built machines, the OAW Albatrosses had a rectangular footstep in the nose, ostensibly to assist ground access to the engine, although simple ladders were often used. Due to higher ambient air temperatures as compared with northern France, this D.III has two radiators.

Gleaming and glossy, Albatros D.III(Oef) 53.21 shows off its sleek lines. The second D.III Oeffag produced, this machine displays a fat and borderless fuselage cross that would be seen on only a few other D.III(Oef)s. Engine is fully cowled, wheel spokes are exposed, and wing root fairings are metal.

began arriving in summer and fought concurrently with the Johannisthal D.IIIs and D.Vs. German researcher Reinhard Zankl submits that subsequent D.III(OAW) production batches featured 238 machines (D.2362–2599/17), 200 machines (D.3056–3255/17), and then 200 more (D.5022–5221/17), for 838 total machines; 338 machines more than the D.IIIs made by Johannisthal.

Along with Albatros and OAW, the Oesterreichische Flugzeugfabrik AG (Austrian Aircraft Factory, or Oeffag) received a production order in December 1916 for 20 Albatros D.IIs for use with the Austro-Hungarian Army Königlich und Kaiserlich Luftfahrtruppen (Royal and Imperial Air Service, or LFT). Of these 20 machines, 16 were built (53.01–53.16) before Oeffag's production focus also shifted to the D.III. Physically these D.III(Oef) machines resembled their German brethren, save for a few noteworthy exceptions. The first was the 185Ps Austro-Daimler Dm 185; an in-line, water-cooled, six-cylinder engine, fully enshrouded within metal cowl panels through which a coolant pipe protruded to the wing-mounted Daimler radiator. Later these cowls were removed to expose the cylinder heads to the slipstream and facilitate engine

Oeffag-built D.IIIs served postwar in the Polish Air Force. Here one features Oeffag's redesigned rounded nose and spinner-less propeller, both of which resulted in a marked increase in speed. The German D.III design never followed Oeffag's lead, although photographs show at least one D.V so shaped, as well as later Albatros prototypes that never reached production.

cooling. This engine was heavier than the 160Ps Mercedes D.III and required lengthening the wing chord 10cm to increase wing surface area, although when the wing failure of Johannisthal-built machines became known, Oeffag engineers found ways to avoid the problem. This led to more solid ribs constructed of heavier plywood, spar flange thickness doubled at points of stress, and metal reinforcements fitted between the spar and the front stringer, which at its fuselage juncture was prevented from twisting by a metal fitting. But while they avoided the catastrophe of wing failures, initially the Austrian machines were hamstrung with delays due to finding a suitable propeller for use with the more powerful 185Ps engine.

D.III(Oef) armament consisted of a single synchronized 8mm Schwarzlose M07/12, internally mounted to starboard of the longitudinal axis; some machines also had one to port. A blast tube connected to the barrel and extended through the engine compartment to prevent the accidental ignition of any accumulated gasses within. This enclosed arrangement helped keep the gun better heated than if it had been mounted externally, but it also eliminated in-flight accessibility. Later armament increased to two guns, which became standard with D.III(Oef)s.

Oeffag production occurred in three series. Series 53 was comprised of 45 185Ps machines, 53.20–53.64. Series 153 was comprised of 281 200Ps machines, 153.01–153.281, within which a redesign replaced the spinner with a rounded nose after German wind tunnel tests had shown that this improved propeller efficiency and increased speed by some 14km/h (9mph). Although implemented on some later Albatros D prototypes, no Johannisthal and OAW D-types utilized such a configuration. (There are photographs of one German Albatros so configured, but it is not known if this was done in-field or at the factory.) Series 253 was contracted in May 1918 and comprised of 260 machines of 225Ps, 253.01–253.260. Cream of the Albatros D.III crop, Oeffag's Series 253 machines were enthusiastically received. Quotes compiled by German researcher Peter Grosz reveal pilots regarded their Series 253 machines as "first class and superior to any fighter"; "equal to all combat requirements"; and "meets every demand, is solid and well-constructed, climbs rapidly and is preferred … because of its peerless flight characteristics."

Albatros fighters under construction at the Oeffag facility in Wiener-Neustadt. Distant machines are D.IIs, while the majority are new D.IIIs, including the first, 53.20. At first glance the varying stages of completeness appear somewhat random, but machines at left have engines and wheels installed. The stockpile of wings in the right foreground suggests pending installation.

Excluding prototypes, Albatros, OAW, and Oeffag built a total of 1,924 Albatros D.IIIs. After their introduction to Western Front service at the end of December 1916, the D.III/D.III(OAW)'s front-line inventory steadily rose during 1917 and peaked at 446 at the end of October and then declined slowly to 357 at the end of February 1918, after which its inventory plummeted to fewer than 20 by the start of May, with numbers never rebounding above 100 for the rest of the war as the type was superseded by the Fokker D.VII. The 586 Albatros D.III(Oef)s saw Eastern and Italian Front service with various Fliegerkompagnien (Flying Companies, or Fliks) beginning in June 1917, and served throughout the war. In August 1918, front-line inventories contained 142 Series 153 D.IIIs and 66 Series 253 D.IIIs; Series 53 had been relegated to the status of a front-line trainer.

TECHNICAL SPECIFICATIONS

The cornerstone of the Johannisthal and OAW-built Albatros D-types was the 160Ps Daimler Mercedes F-1466 engine, commonly known as the Mercedes D.III. "D" signified it was a product of Daimler Motoren Gesellschaft, Stuttgart-Untertürkheim, and "III" was a Roman numeral that Idflieg assigned to signify performance range ("0" was under 80Ps; "I" was 80–100Ps; "II" was 100–150Ps; "III" was 150–200Ps). It was a normally aspirated, direct-drive, water-cooled, carbureted, in-line, overhead-cam, six-cylinder engine, cowled within detachable metal panels. Fuel tanks were located immediately aft; there was no firewall. Pilot engine-management included a throttle mounted on the control column; a spark-retarding lever on the port cockpit wall, along with an engine magneto switch key and starting magneto crank; and an auxiliary throttle, located port-forward in the cockpit. Cooling was provided by a single radiator centrally mounted within the upper wing that was plumbed externally to carry coolant to and from the engine, and later this radiator was repositioned slightly to starboard. This solid and reliable engine enabled the D.III to attain a maximum speed of 175km/h (109mph) and climb to 5,000 meters (15,250 feet) in 30 minutes.

As are all performance specifications, these figures are illustrative, not finite, and are usually generated via a test pilot flying a new airplane in optimum weather conditions. Real-world conditions with aging airframes, hard-flown engines, and neophyte pilots flying on a hot and humid day would produce less than handbook performance.

The Mercedes D.III engine traced its roots to the 1913 Mercedes D.I engine, a 190kg (dry weight) in-line, water-cooled engine with six cylinders cast in pairs atop an aluminum crankcase, serviced by an overhead cam and two Bosch magnetos for dual ignition redundancy. Airplanes employing the Mercedes D.I included the LVG B.I and Albatros B.II. The following year brought the Mercedes D.II, which featured an increased bore from 120 to 125mm and increased stroke from 140 to

Mercedes D.III engine in a new Albatros D.III of unknown serial number, from either the 600- or 750-series. Rocker arm boxes are located directly above each cylinder. Fuel-tank air-pressure pump protrudes at front. Sprung footstep, access hatches, and louvers are pristine – the latter are often crushed by ground-crew ladders.

Port-side drawing of a 160Ps Mercedes D.III. (A) Hot air pipe; (B) propeller hub; (C) carburetor float casing; (D) carburetor; (E) spark plug cable insulation tube; (F) camshaft pressurized oil pipe; (G) priming petcock; (H) spark plugs; (I) intake manifold; (J) cooling water pipe; (K) camshaft housing; (L) carburetor hot water supply; (M) air pump; (N) decompression lever; (O) cooling water pump; (P) magneto; (Q) carburetor heating pipe; (R) ignition timing adjustment mechanism; (S) oil pump; (T) oil drain valve.

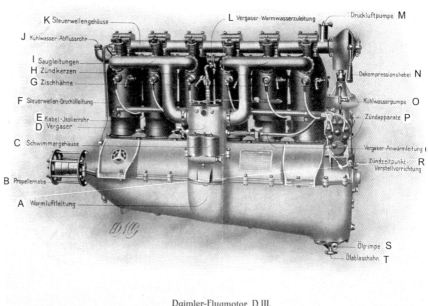

Daimler-Flugmotor D III.
Vergaserseite.

150mm, increasing power output to 120Ps. The cylinders were still paired, although the cam tower was now enclosed and dry weight increased slightly to 210kg. Airplanes employing the Mercedes D.II included the LVG B.I, Albatros B.I and B.II, and Fokker D.I.

In 1915 Daimler developed the Mercedes D.III. Pressed sheet steel water jackets were welded to steel cylinders now bolted individually to a two-piece (upper and lower) sloped aluminum crankcase. These bolts passed through the upper crankcase half to attach to the lower, which not only secured the cylinders but aided securing the crankcase halves. Each cylinder featured single intake and exhaust ports and contained a four-ring piston machined from steel forgings; the compression ratio was 4.5:1. The valve gear was contained within six aluminum-capped boxes through which rocker arms protruded to engage the intake and exhaust valves; these boxes were aligned above each cylinder and bolted to the camshaft. A two-barrel, twin-jet, updraft, float-type carburetor was positioned on the port side of the engine between the third and fourth cylinders and enclosed within a cast aluminum water jacket to prevent induction icing. Each carburetor throat fed a fuel–air mixture to three cylinders via branched steel tube intake manifolds that were often covered with asbestos cord lagging and bound with tape to prevent heat loss. Both throats were interconnected to the throttle but there was no altitude-compensating mixture control for the pilot. Carburetor air intakes on the starboard side of the lower crankcase enabled internal oil cooling fins to warm the incoming air, further prevented induction icing. Fuel flow to the carburetor was initiated via a cylindrical camshaft-driven air pump that pressurized the main and emergency fuel tanks (80 and 23 liters, or 21.1 and 6.1 gallons, respectively) located between the engine and the cockpit. Two Bosch Z.H.6 magnetos were affixed to the rear of the engine and driven by bevel gears off the vertical jackshaft that connected to the camshaft; the speed of the magnetos was 1.5 times that of the engine. Two Bosch spark plugs were fitted to each cylinder below the intake, and exhaust valves and

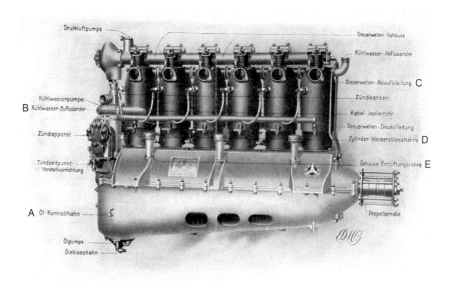

Starboard-side drawing of a 160Ps Mercedes D.III. Most of the details are the same as found on the port side, except for (A) Oil control valve; (B) cooling water inlet pipe; (C) camshaft oil drain; (D) cylinder water drain cocks; (E) crankcase ventilation pipes.

Daimler-Flugmotor D III.
Auspuffseite.

their associated wiring was routed through fiber tubes affixed horizontally to the cylinders. Cylinder firing order was 1, 5, 3, 6, 2, 4.

Engine cooling for the Albatros D.III was provided by a Teeves and Braun wing-mounted radiator that was centrally located between the D.II's central N-struts and connected to the engine fore and aft via externally plumbed pipes; the fore pipe was plumbed down the starboard side of the engine and connected to the first cylinder water jacket. In the second half of the first production batch the radiator was relocated to starboard – although still within the center-section struts – ostensibly to reduce "top-hamper" disrupting the pilot's aiming line-of-sight, although all Oeffag radiators retained their central locations. To facilitate cooling in hotter climes, such as in Palestine, D.IIIs and D.III(OAW)s were equipped with two airfoil radiators, one each port and starboard.

For coolant, Daimler recommended that soft water (water free of minerals, particularly lime, which can foul plumbing) be used and specified the allowance of pure rainwater, boiled water, or distilled water; all had to be filtered prior to use. During cold weather, hot water was to be used with glycerin or denatured alcohol added; a 60–70 percent blend of glycerin lowered the freezing point of water to -36°F (-37.8°C). Coolant circulation was via a water

Mercedes D.III (D-1466) Engine Specifications	
Bore	140mm
Stroke	160mm
Compression ratio	4.50:1
Average bhp and speed	162.5 at 1,400rpm
Total dry engine weight*	618lb
Weight per bhp	3.80lb
Fuel consumption per hour	11.75gal
Direction of propeller rotation	clockwise
*Excludes propeller hub and exhaust manifold.	

pump located above the magnetos and driven off the vertical jackshaft, with pump lubrication conducted by hand via a pilot-controlled, screw-down grease lubricator.

All engine parts were lubricated with oil supplied by an oil pump driven by the lower vertical jackshaft at the bottom rear of the engine. The main oil circuit fed the crankshaft and camshaft bearings while a supplementary circuit drew fresh oil from the oil tank and continually fed it into the system. An auxiliary suction pump drew oil away from the system and returned it to the oil tank.

Engine access for maintenance and servicing was somewhat limited by the close engine cowling, but these panels could be removed easily and had a round hatch to port that allowed access to the carburetor, as did a hatch on the port fuselage. The starboard engine cowl had no access hatch but there was one below on the fuselage, and several hatches under the nose granted access to the carburetor air intakes, oil drain, oil line, and oil pump on the bottom of the engine. Also, six staggered metal louvres – three each on the nose, port and starboard – promoted airflow circulation through the engine compartment to remove excess heat and prevent potentially volatile gasses from accumulating.

After examining a 160Ps Mercedes D.III engine from a captured Albatros D.I, the January 13, 1916 issue of the British aero-weekly *Flight* stated the following:

> If we are not altogether enamoured of the design … the workmanship and finish embodied in the Mercedes are, on the other hand, such as to excite admiration, for they are certainly of the very finest. Moreover … it is very evident that reliability almost to the exclusion of all else has been the object sought after. This is revealed by the "heftiness" of every internal working part; even in the reciprocating members little or no effort seems to have been made to cut down weight to an extent likely to influence reliability. On the contrary, it is clear the designers have, as we suggested above, been content to limit revolutions, and by doing so take the advantage permitted to increase the factor of safety, the result being that the Mercedes – as it undoubtedly is – is an engine comparable with an ordinary car engine in the matter of infrequent need for attention and overhaul, long life, and unfailing service except for accident.
>
> It must not be thought from this, however, that the question of weight reduction has not received any consideration whatever. On the contrary, it has evidently been carefully studied, although this is a fact that is not by any means obvious from the

Austro-Daimler 200Ps Engine Specifications	
Bore	135mm
Stroke	175mm
Compression ratio	5.02:1
Average bhp and speed	200 at 1,400rpm
Total dry engine weight*	728.5lb
Weight per bhp	3.64lb
Fuel consumption per hour	13.88gal
Direction of propeller rotation	clockwise

exterior. It is in respect to the parts that may be considered as the framework rather than the working parts of the engine that the endeavours in this direction have been directed, especially the crankcase and the cylinders, though nowhere has the achievement of the object been allowed to interfere with the rigidity of the engine as a whole, and therefore with its smooth running potentialities.

In early 1917 the Mercedes piston heads were redesigned from concave to flat, with a resultant increase in cylinder compression that generated 175Ps, but it is difficult to establish which particular Albatros airframes were outfitted with the stronger engine. Both the 160 and 175Ps engines were identical outwardly; new engines could be retrofitted into older machines; and already-purchased 160Ps engines had to be used prior to production use of 175Ps engines. For example, the D.III(OAW) test flown on June 9, 1917 was equipped with a 160Ps Mercedes.

The Mercedes D.III turned a fixed-pitch, two-blade, wooden propeller consisting of several 6–20mm-thick boards that had been glued together so that the grain of each board ran diagonally to the next, which prevented twisting. Preferred woods included walnut, ash, mahogany, and teak, but eventual import shortages necessitated also using maple, elm, and pine. The latter was avoided because as a softwood it was too sensitive to rain, hail, sand, and dust erosion; if used, pine required special protection. During construction the various wood laminations were heated to 100°F (38°C) to enhance the permeability of the freshly made animal glue, which after application was allowed to penetrate the wood before the laminations were clamped together for 24 hours. Afterwards the center bore hole and bolt holes were drilled to better than a half-millimeter accuracy, the adherence to which was especially important for use with machine-gun synchronization systems. The propeller blades were shaped by hand using guide templates to ensure accuracy, sanded, and then received multiple coats of shellac and varnish. Shellac is not waterproof and was likely used to seal the wood grain as an undercoat for the varnish, which protected the propeller from delamination due to moisture.

Mercedes radiator in detail. Water heated by the engine cylinders was piped up to the radiator and circulated between over 2,000 square tubes connected at their ends, through which flowed passing air. The combined surface area of these tubes cooled the liquid which then returned to the engine. The radiator sides reveal that the tubes were angled backwards to best utilize airflow through the wing. The vertical tank accommodated coolant expansion without overflow.

Axial propellers were commonly seen on the Albatros D.III, as were those of Garuda and Wolff, but regardless of manufacturer the propeller hubs were enclosed within a large aerodynamic spinner (of a slightly smaller diameter than the fuselage to allow the entry of cooling air into the engine compartment) that could be removed for preventative or reparative maintenance access. Idflieg's 1916 *Propellermerkbuch* (Propeller Notebook) stipulated that all propellers were to be kept clean, with the wood and metal parts greased strongly for moisture protection, especially in damp weather and after flights in fog or rain. Problems lurked even in good weather:

In continuously dry weather the wood of the propeller shrinks; in damp weather it expands. After each weather change therefore the propeller should be examined to see if it sits correctly on the engine hub. If necessary, the nuts on the mounting bolts are to be tightened. If the weather is damp, then the bolts are to be loosened, then retightened correctly, otherwise the propeller can crack by the expansion of the wood at the hub or damage the mounting bolts.

Additionally, flight damage from raindrops or hail and erosion from sand and small pebbles picked up during ground operations degraded propeller performance and required the damaged blade be "sanded off and repainted on the aircraft, an easy task." This led to the dark appearance of some propellers, although photographs also revealed that between sorties the propeller blades were often ensconced within protective sheaths. More significant damage to the leading and trailing edges of propellers could be repaired via a wooden plug that was glued into a trapezoidal excision of the damaged portion of the blade, with the wider portion of the wedge-shaped plug closer to the blade's center to prevent the plug from flying out due to rotational forces. The notebook also stated the following:

… the 160Ps Mercedes engines have a critical period at 1,320 to 1,340rpm when the engine vibrates strongly. With these engines one selects carefully propellers that can make 1,400 to 1,460rpm in flight. If a suitable propeller is not to hand, then one can cut off without hesitation up to 3cm of each blade. Reducing the diameter by around 1cm increases the speed by 6 to 10rpm. With smooth running engines this measure is not necessary.

The Albatros D.III and D.III(OAW)'s armament consisted of two fixed and forward-firing Maxim lMG 08/15 7.92mm air-cooled machine guns, each synchronized to fire 500 rounds through the propeller arc. Colloquially known as a "Spandau" due to its manufacture at Königlich Gewehr und Munitions Fabrik (Royal Gun and Munitions Factory), Spandau, Berlin, the weapon's lineage traces back to its 1884 invention by Hiram Maxim, an American from Sangerville, Maine, who worked in London and eventually became a naturalized British subject. His machine gun utilized a belt-fed and recoil-operated design in which the barrel and bolt recoiled together a few millimeters before the barrel stopped and the bolt continued rearward to extract and eject the fired cartridge and cock the firing pin. A return spring pushed the bolt back toward the breech, chambering the next cartridge and locking in place to be fired again.

The Maxim and its variants saw greatest use by the German Army, which adopted the weapon as the MG 08, in its standard 7.92x57mm (measurements of the cartridge case) military rifle caliber. In 1915, upon aviation's practice of fixing machine guns to airplanes and synchronizing them to fire forward through a spinning propeller arc, the Maxim's precise firing made it an ideal weapon for this purpose. However, being that it was originally water-cooled, the weight associated with the water-jacketed barrel was detrimental to airplane performance and required a conversion to air-cooling. The seemingly obvious solution was to remove the water jacket, but since it supported the barrel as it moved back and forth during firing, the jacket was instead drained of water and its front and sides perforated to allow the circulation of cooling air. Subsequent designs included removing unnecessary parts and replacing the water jacket with a perforated jacket of reduced diameter. This weapon became known as the lMG 08/15.

The weapon was synchronized to fire 500 rounds between the rotating propeller blades at a maximum rate of 450 rounds per minute, but one must remember that this rate was dependent upon engine speed and varied with different propeller rpms as the synchronization gear compensated for the variable frequency with which the blades passed before the gun muzzles. The standard synchronization gear used by German airplane manufacturers was the Fokker *Zentralsteuerung* (central control) system. This was a natural progression from the initial *Stangensteuerung* (pushrod control) system, which was actually an "interrupter gear" comprised of pushrods and mechanical linkages driven by a rotating cam connected to the engine crankshaft or camshaft that prevented (interrupted) the weapon from firing whenever the blades passed before the muzzle. The *Zentralsteuerung* system replaced the rigid pushrods – which were susceptible to contraction due to frigid temperatures at altitude – with a flexible drive shaft that rotated a cam and engaged a spring-loaded pin that pushed the trigger, permitting gunfire

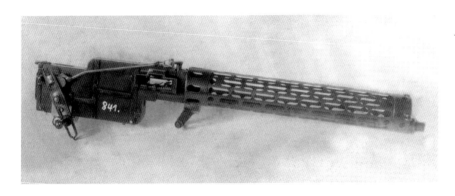

A Maxim lMG 08/15 machine gun with belted 7.62mm ammunition. All Albatros D models were equipped with two of these weapons synchronized to fire through the propeller arc. Maximum firing rate was 450 rounds per minute, although this changed with the variable speed of the propeller blades.

synchronized with moments when the blades were clear, as opposed to an interrupter system preventing gunfire when the blades were not clear. The end result was the same, although synchronization was more reliable and efficient than interruption.

Despite the Fokker *Zentralsteuerung* system being furnished to all German airplane manufacturers, Albatros chose instead to devise and utilize an in-house two-gun synchronization mechanism that comprised a cam and oscillating rods, designed by Werkmeister Hedtke and eventually modified by Werkmeister Semmler. This decision raised Idflieg's concerns that multiple synchronization systems would complicate armorer training, but Albatros remained committed to the Hedtke system, having apparently tested Fokker's *Zentralsteuerung* system in October 1916 and deemed said testing to be unsuccessful. Still, Idflieg considered the *Zentralsteuerung* system to be superior.

Standard armament for Oeffag machines was the M07/12 machine gun, which unfortunately had its share of problems. It was a retarded blowback gun, and so the expanding propellant gasses forced the cartridge case backwards out of the chamber. This required the bolt be free to move backwards and thus it was unlocked from the barrel and held in place via a recoil spring and inertia. An elbow joint attached to the bolt that retarded its initial rearward movement and delayed opening the breech until the bullet had exited the barrel, but the powerful cartridges used still caused the breech to

Albatros D.III(Oef) 153.181 with and without cowlings. The engine was closely cowled, although a small blister was needed to fit over the forward end of the intake manifold. The Schwarzlose guns have been raised, with a spent shell ejection chute between the fuel filler neck access and fuel valve access doors.

Business end of an Oeffag D.III, which somewhat resembles the hull of modern nuclear submarines. The fully cowled engine is evident, with a radiator pipe leading back to the central radiator; radiators were never offset to starboard on Oeffag machines. Two blast tubes protrude out front, slightly higher than the stubby exhaust pipes.

Subtle differences between Albatros and OAW-built D.IIIs, clockwise from top left: Albatros machine from first production batch, with Mercedes D.III and central radiator; 600- or 750-series Albatros, with rectangular nose footstep; OAW-built D.III in Palestine, with nose step, two radiators, and associated plumbing down either side of the Mercedes D.III; and an OAW D.III, with a Mercedes D.IIIa engine, identifiable by offset rocker arm boxes and fat air-pump cylinder. Note that Johannisthal-built Albatros front panel lines extend to the leading edge of the wings, while OAW lines extend beyond to the wing spar.

open too early. The barrel was shortened to allow the bullet to leave before the breech opened, but this reduced muzzle velocity and required a heavy bolt that limited rate of fire to 400 rounds per minute. Furthermore, the weapon was adversely affected by pressure changes that hampered the rate of fire and caused the weapon to stop firing when above 3,000 meters. Modifications to combat these problems led to the eventual development of the Schwarzlose M16.

Triggers on all Albatrosses were centrally located on the control column and situated so the guns could be fired separately or simultaneously. Gun breeches were pilot accessible for cocking and clearing jams. Hemp-belted cartridges were stored in magazines forward the cockpit and fed to the guns via curved metal chutes. After passing through the guns, the empty belts descended separate chutes (which on the port side was covered by an aerodynamic fairing [a "*Beule*", or bump] on Johannisthal machines, although this *Beule* was absent on OAW builds) to collect in bins adjacent the magazines; cartridge cases were ejected overboard. As with the engines, the guns were

Depiction of how an angled scarf joint increased surface area to be glued, resulting in a stronger bond than if the pieces had been glued via an end-on butt joint. Albatros seams were reinforced internally with fabric and did not necessarily align with formers when glued and nailed to the airframe.

partially cowled within detachable metal panels. On Oeffag airplanes the guns were enclosed ("buried") within the fuselage and fired through port and starboard blast tubes that straddled the engine. During production of Series 153 machines, experiments were conducted with the guns raised more to eye-level to improve aiming, but this relocation proved unpopular when pilots complained about reduced visibility and gun oil hitting their faces.

Johannisthal, OAW, and Oeffag Albatros D.III fuselages featured a circular nose and slab-sided cross-section that faired smoothly into an ovoid top and underside, with the ovoid transitions becoming more knife-edged as they neared the empennage. The intersection of the curved belly and slab-sided fuselage at the lower wing leading- and trailing-edge connection points created drag-producing protuberances that required the installation of either wood or metal aerodynamic fairings, the shapes of which varied between manufacturers. The fuselage was of semi-monocoque construction, whereby the external skin acted in concert with the frame to share the stress of external loads, resulting in great strength without the need for internal wire bracing. The wooden frame employed six longerons, three each port and starboard. The center longerons were L-sections forward of the cockpit and spruce rectangular sections from there aft. The upper and lower longerons were largely ash L-sections up to the cockpit, with spruce employed from there aft, along which ground wires were channeled rearwards from the engine mounts to the cabane strut mounts (which channeled the ground to a wire in the upper wing), tail-post tube, and horizontal stabilizer. Connected to the longerons were thick simple transverse formers spaced approximately every 2 feet, with four transverse supports employed as engine bearers forward of the cockpit. The entire frame was treated for moisture protection.

Covering this frame was a sectioned 2–3mm three-ply birch plywood skin that had been pressed into compound shapes in molds and then glued together via beveled scarf-joints that increased the surface area to be glued, providing a stronger connection than if the two pieces had been simply glued end-to-end. These scarf-jointed seams were internally reinforced with glued strips of heavy-weave cotton fabric, and the resultant large shells were then glued and nailed to the formers and stringers, with the corners secured by screws. Glue was the primary bond for joining the structure; the steel nails and screws were used to hold the structure in place as the glue cured, but they also provided additional strength. When attached to the frame the scarf-joint seams did not necessarily align with the locations of the formers and typically were offset. Both sides of the skin received multiple coats of shellac and varnish, producing the oft-noted "warm straw yellow" appearance and gleaming high-gloss sheen.

The Albatros D.III employed a high-sided, ovoid-shaped open cockpit, with edges strengthened by a double-thickness of wood and covered with a padded leather coaming, with a small windscreen forward that shielded the pilot from the slipstream. Entry was assisted by a single rounded sprung-door footstep located on the lower port longeron, although normally pilots gained the cockpit via a ladder and ground crew assistance, and it is reasonable to speculate that the footstep was meant more as a means of exit assistance rather than entry. Early machines of the first Johannisthal production batch had rounded footsteps,

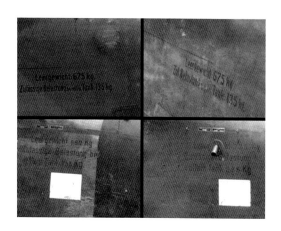

A few variations of Albatros and OAW-built D.III weights tables; the top two are Albatros machines, the bottom two OAW. The white squares are rigging diagrams. OAW weights tables are higher up on the cockpit and collocated with Idflieg and manufacturer placards. *"Leergewicht: 675 kg. Zulässige Belastung bei vollem Tank: 135 kg."* means "Empty [airplane] weight: 675 kg. Permissible load at full [fuel] tank: 135 kg." The tube at right was a common field modification for firing flare guns from the cockpit.

but after D.2108/16 they had been replaced by rectangular steps. All subsequent Johannisthal and OAW machines had rectangular steps, with the 600- and 750-series Johannisthal machines and all OAW-builds having an additional nose footstep near the front of the engine that ostensibly aided ground crew. All Oeffag machines had no nose step and employed a rounded footstep for cockpit entry and exit.

The cockpit interior was much more spacious and protective from the elements than those of concurrent French and British machines, and the lack of a firewall enabled the Albatros pilots to enjoy the warming benefits of radiant engine heat. The pilot sat in an upholstered bucket seat adjustable fore and aft with security provided by a four-point seatbelt and shoulder harness restraint, although instead of securing the pilot directly across his legs the wide seatbelt fastened across the top of the bucket seat. This helped prevent him from falling from the machine, but the shoulder harness provided the bulk of pilot security. Control of pitch and roll was conducted via a metal control column with two wooden hand grips that straddled the left and right machine-gun triggers, allowing them to be engaged via the thumbs. Cables leading to the guns were plumbed externally from the column's hollow core, as was the cable leading to the primary engine throttle clamped to the left hand grip; on Oeffag machines the throttle was located on the starboard cockpit wall. There was no trim to relieve the pilot of any control pressures, but a locking device on the control column could be engaged to permit a brief measure of hands-off flying, by preventing fore and aft control movement (elevator control) while still allowing lateral movement (aileron control). A conventional rudder bar with metal toe straps enabled control of yaw about the vertical axis, although there were neither toe brakes, nor rudder trim, nor tailskid steering.

Flight and navigation instrumentation in the Johannisthal and OAW Albatros cockpit was sparse, especially when compared with RFC machines; there was no "instrument panel" as is commonplace today. Instead, a centrally located tachometer attached to the metal support of the Maxim breeches, a fuel pressure gauge was behind and to the right of that frame, and a fuel quantity gauge was located on the starboard cockpit wall. An altimeter and airspeed indicator could be present (the latter was an anemometer type and commonly but not exclusively located on an interplane strut) but these were retrofitted installations and not factory standard. The sole navigational instrument was a floor-mounted magnetic compass. This was a less than ideal location for navigating via precise headings but Albatros pilots did not conduct long-range A-to-B navigation often. Instead, they employed pilotage (using fixed visual ground references [roads, lakes, woods, railroads, villages] to guide oneself to a destination) for local short-range navigation over known territories and locales – they were hunting enemy airplanes in a familiar geographical area, not homing cross-country on distant locales across the horizon. Thus the compass mostly provided a measure of general orientation, such as could be useful after a combat melee during which navigation had been ignored in favor of fighting and survival; a pilot could reference the compass and turn in the general direction of home until such time as he identified local landmarks familiar to him.

What the Albatros lacked in flight instrumentation it made up for with fuel and engine controls, three of which were mounted on the port cockpit wall. The first was the engine magneto switch key, which was attached to a chain and removable for safety; in some photographs it can be seen dangling outside the cockpits of parked machines. This switch could be placed in four positions: at position "0" the engine-driven magnetos and the starting magneto were off; at position "M1" (for starting) the left magneto and starting magneto were on; at position "M2" the left magneto was off, while the right magneto and starting magneto were on; and in position "2" both engine-driven magnetos and the starting magneto were on. Next to the magneto switch key was the spark-retarding lever. Often mistaken for the throttle, this lever allowed the pilot to delay the timing of when the spark plugs fired, compensating for slower piston travel at idling or low engine speeds compared with piston speeds at cruise or full-power settings. Forward and below this lever was the starting magneto crank. Although the Albatros D.III required ground assistance for engine starts, it did not employ personnel to "swing" the propeller as did

C

1. JOHANNISTHAL-BUILT ALBATROS D.III RUDDER

The Albatros D.III rudder frame was comprised of steel tube construction and featured – as had the D.I and D.II before it – a vertical trailing edge. The covering fabric was either clear doped linen or painted one of the wing's camouflage colors, with an Albatros company logo affixed to the upper aft quadrant of the rudder.

2. OAW-BUILT ALBATROS D.III RUDDER

An identifying visual hallmark of the OAW-built Albatros D.III was the rounded trailing edge of its rudder, which contrasted with the vertical trailing edge of a Johannisthal build. This configuration lessened the significant bends required to form the vertical trailing edge of the D.III and remained a feature of Albatros D.Vs and D.Vas.

3. FIRST PRODUTION SERIES NOSE

The forward fuselages of Albatros D-types remained fairly consistent, comprised mostly of wood with metal quick-release removable engine panels. First production series machines had horizontal panel lines back to the leading edge of the wings, manufacturer and Idflieg placards, two engine access hatches, and three louvres to promote airflow through the compartment that helped cool the engine and remove any accumulated gases.

4. 600- AND 750-SERIES NOSE

Later Albatros D.IIIs featured forward fuselage details that matched those of the first production batch, save for the addition of a rectangular sprung footstep mounted high and forward on the port fuselage. There was not a corresponding hatch to starboard. Ground crew frequently leaned ladders against the nose for prolonged engine access (a practice that often flattened the louvres) and the new footstep aided ladder use. It also obviated ladder use, whereby a deft crewman could hold the cabane strut, step up on the landing gear strut, and reach the footstep with his left foot and use it for support.

5. ALBATROS D.III(OAW) NOSE

Similar to its Johannisthal brethren, including the nose footstep. The biggest differences were that its horizontal panel lines were situated differently and extended further aft, past the leading edge of the wing to the aft cabane connection point. The manufacturer and Idflieg placards were relocated to the fuselage near the cockpit, and the engine cowl panels featured a "crease" along their bottom edges.

6. ALBATROS D.III(OEF) NOSE

Oeffag Albatros noses initially resembled those of German-built machines but gradually the spinner was removed, and ultimately the nose section redesigned into a rounded shape that somewhat resembles a modern submarine hull. This had the benefit of increasing airspeed. The fuselage had the usual louvres and hatches but more of the latter, allowing access to the fuel tanks and fuel control valves on the port side of the cockpit.

7. ALBATROS D.III TWIN RADIATORS

Both Johannisthal and OAW built D.IIIs with twin radiators to – obviously – increase cooling, particularly in warmer theaters such as Palestine. Normally each radiator was served by its own plumbing that ran down the port and starboard sides of the engine, but some machines utilized the normal single pipe connected to a "U-shaped" fitting, with each end connected to a different radiator.

1

2

3

4

5

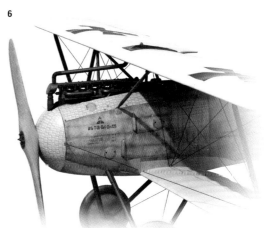

6

7

airplanes with rotary engines. Instead, ground crew filled the cylinder petcocks with a mixture of oil and benzene, slowly pulled the propeller through several complete revolutions to draw the priming fuel into the cylinders, and then the pilot positioned the magneto switch key to M1 and rapidly hand-cranked the starting magneto. This created a continuous spark discharge in the cylinder at or past top dead center, igniting the fuel–air mixture and driving the piston downward. This action caused the engine-driven magnetos to fire the spark plugs in the other cylinders, starting the engine and engaging the engine-driven air pump that continuously pressurized the fuel tank to send fuel to the carburetor, thereby completing the self-sustaining cycle.

The front of the Albatros cockpit was comprised mostly of the cartridge belt container and ammunition storage bins, but protruding from the upper left side was an auxiliary throttle handle, which was a horizontal metal rod with a looped end. In the event of primary throttle control abnormality (e.g. if the control cable were severed by enemy bullets), the pilot could push the auxiliary throttle fully forward until a detent at the end of the rod locked the auxiliary throttle to the carburetor, thereby restoring throttle control.

Fuel control valves were located on the right side of the cockpit, where a wooden panel supported a fuel pressure

ABOVE Subtle differences between Oeffag-built D.IIIs. Top: Albatros Series 53 machine 53.21 shows that Oeffag initially retained the same shape used by German D.IIIs, although as shown here the entire engine could be enclosed, with openings for a truncated exhaust manifold. Bottom: Tests revealed removing the spinner and rounding the nose increased top speed significantly, so from 152.112 the Oeffag's D.IIIs were so constructed.

RIGHT Wing gap comparison between an Albatros D.II (top) and D.III (bottom). To improve pilot vision up and forward, the D.I's gap had been lowered significantly for the D.II. When the D.III was produced, the gap was increased again but remained less than what was used on the D.I.

gauge valve control, an air pump selector valve, a fuel tank air pressure valve, and a fuel tank flow selector valve. For normal engine start and flight procedures these valve handles all pointed downward and required little pilot attention. However, the pilot was afforded a measure of flexibility between the main and emergency fuel tanks if the need arose. Setting the fuel tank air pressure valve to "Emergency Tank" and the fuel tank flow selector valve to "Emergency Fuel" enabled fuel to flow from the emergency tank to the carburetor. Moving the fuel tank flow selector valve to "Emergency Fuel Filling" allowed fuel to flow to the carburetor but also the main tank, where total fuel quantity could be read from the fuel gauge that measured the main tank only (assuming pilots trusted this gauge was accurate). Below the fuel valve panel a hand-operated air pump allowed the pilot to pressurize the fuel tanks for starting (prior to pressurization from the engine-driven air pump) or when the engine-driven air pump was inoperative. Lastly, a water pump greaser was installed on the far starboard side that the pilot twisted a half-turn every ten minutes to ensure proper water pump lubrication. Incidentally, while fuel tank location and access between the cockpit and engine required the removal of engine cowl panels of Johannisthal and OAW machines, Oeffag installed a much more convenient fuel filler access panel on the port fuselage, near the aft center-section strut connection point.

Oeffag cockpit configuration was slightly different, with the fuel controls situated along the port cockpit wall, externally accessible via a metal hatch; an altimeter and a tachometer at the front of the cockpit on either side of the Schwarzlose breech blocks, with engine magneto and starting magneto switches located at bottom right; and a combined throttle and spark-retardant control handle was affixed to the starboard cockpit wall.

Lift for the Albatros D.III was provided by two equal and constant chord, wooden-framed, wire-braced, subtly tip-tapered, single-bay wings of slightly unequal span. These were covered with a skin of doped fabric and affixed to the airplane with positive stagger but without dihedral or sweepback, although the trailing edges of the ailerons were raked slightly aft. The frame consisted of two fabric-bound, rectangular wooden spars situated approximately 2 feet 8 inches apart, held in alignment via steel compression bars (to which a ground wire was attached) and turnbuckle-adjusted cross wires. The basswood ribs were capped with ash, employed prodigious lightening holes, and were situated 16¼ inches apart on the upper wing and 13¾ inches apart on the lower wings, between which intermediate ribs extended back to the aft main spar. The ribs were joined by a span-wise rounded cap strip to form

Empennage comparison between a Johannisthal-built Albatros D.III, top, and D.III(OAW), bottom. The main difference is the rounded trailing edge of the OAW rudder, on which the company logo was more angled and oriented to "fly away" from the nose. OAW fuselage cross placement is further forward than found on Johannisthal machines, with the white borders thicker and the black crosses thinner. Both machines are sans serial number on the vertical stabilizer, but normally this was not true for Johannisthal-built machines.

the leading edge, and their ends were connected via an approximately 1mm-thick wire that formed the trailing edge of the wing. The upper and lower wings were connected via pairs of wire-braced interplane struts located outboard port and starboard, one pair on each side. The struts were streamlined steel tube construction and were connected to the upper and lower spars. These spars, as with all wooden components of the wings, were varnished for moisture protection. The lower inboard leading edges of D.III wings displayed a "*Nicht Auftreten*" placard, meaning "do not step." This location was ahead of the spar and could not support a man's weight. Due to the machine's three-point stance and the normal angles of photographs, these placards are not often discernible.

The frame was covered in swatches of linen fabric sewn to 5mm-wide strips of reinforcement tape that had been tied to the upper and lower cap strips of each rib. Stitching was accomplished via overhand loops secured by half hitches, spaced approximately 30mm apart along the ribs; once complete, the stitching was covered by strips of 25mm-wide finishing tape; no finishing tape was used on Oeffag machines. The wings then received applications of dope that weatherproofed the fabric and rendered it taut, causing it to pull against the trailing edge wire and create the classic scalloped appearance associated with many World War I machines. For pilot control of roll, fabric-covered steel frame ailerons were attached to an auxiliary spar located aft of the aft main spar, on the outer port and starboard portions of the upper wing only. Control cables descended vertically behind the aft interplane struts and into the lower wings, through which they were routed to the control column.

The wood-framed empennage featured a ply-covered vertical stabilizer and two fabric-covered horizontal stabilizers, all of which employed curved leading edges and low aspect ratios. The steel-tube-framed, counter-balanced rudder and one-piece elevator were covered with doped fabric and operated via cables routed through the fuselage and into the cockpit. The rudder-post bellcrank and connecting cables were housed completely within the fuselage, and for servicing required the installation of port and starboard access hatches near the trailing edge of the vertical stabilizer, above the horizontal stabilizers. The empennage undersurface featured a wood-framed and three-ply skinned

Tailskid on an Albatros D.III(Oef). Rounded where bungeed for shock absorption, it became slab-sided at the aft connection point where the steel-shoe began. This shoe enabled tailskids to "plow" into aerodrome turf and soil, helping slow the machine and prevent ground loops.

triangular ventral fin that not only aided lateral stability about the vertical axis but housed a one-piece, steel-shoed, ash tailskid in the "bee-stinger" position that was bungeed for a measure of shock absorption. Due to the need for strength in this area the ventral fin received a dual covering of three-ply birch, which created a total skin thickness of 4mm.

Similarly, the main landing gear employed bungeed shock absorption that also served to connect the struts to the wheel axle, upon which revolved two covered disc wheels with rectangular (Johannisthal), oval (OAW), or round (Oeffag) valve access hatches; a steel restraining cable was used to limit axle travel and prevented gear collapse in the event of bungee failure. The struts were streamlined steel tubes arranged in a conventional V-configuration that inserted into tubular port and starboard sockets bolted and strapped to the curved underside of the fuselage nose, as well as being bolted to the belly between the wings. The rear struts were cable-braced. A transverse tubular tie rod was located behind the axle, and both the axle and tie rod were enclosed within a wooden aerodynamic fairing on OAW and Oeffag Albatrosses.

Performance specifications of the various D.III builds varied between the German and Austrian builds. The D.III and D.III(OAW) were similar machines and thus had similar performances, although the latter's lower wings were more robustly constructed to avoid the structural failures of the early Johannisthal builds. Both were inferior to the Oeffag machines, which across the board employed better and stronger construction; redesigned the front fuselage to increase speed (the Series 153 machines); and used increasingly stronger engines (ultimately 225Ps with the Series 253 machines) that provided greater speed, climb, and ceiling with each new series.

Starboard axle/landing gear strut connection on an Oeffag D.III. The axle fitted inside a wire-braced V-strut and was secured by wrapped bungees that bore the weight of the airplane. The loop above the bungees was a steel restraining cable that supported the machine in case of bungee failure, preventing the strut apex from digging into the ground and overturning the airplane.

Jasta 11 Albatros D.III 624/17 – presumably red, with an unknown-colored tail and repainted serial number – at Roucourt, May 1917. The upper wing camouflage employs the usual three-color scheme and is another example that Albatros used Venetian red on their 600- and 750-series D.IIIs.

Beautiful lineup of Jasta 30 Albatros D.IIIs and early D.Vs. The D.IIIs 760/17 and 767/17 also employed Venetian red with their wing camouflage colors. 791/17 uses two colors, but the lighter color appears darker than the pale green on nearby airplanes. Is it possible that being one of the last 750-series machines built, 791/17 was assembled *after* the Idflieg directive and thus actually has green and mauve wings?

Factory Finishes and Idiosyncracies

Although produced by two different manufacturing companies in Germany that used camouflage variations, both manufacturers produced Albatros D.IIIs with high-gloss shellacked and varnished birch fuselages that have been described as appearing "warm straw yellow." The spinner, engine cowling panels, fittings, access hatches, vents, and cabane/interplane/undercarriage struts were either light gray, pale greenish-gray, or greenish-beige. The wheel covers and undersurfaces of the wings, ailerons, horizontal stabilizers, and elevator were light blue, but the uppersurfaces and national markings varied between the individual manufacturers. Contrastingly, Oeffag-built machines almost universally were not camouflaged at the factory, with unpainted wooden fuselages and all fabric-covered surfaces employing natural linen.

Albatros Flugzeugwerke (D.1910–2309/16; D.600–649/17; D.750–799/17)

Johannisthal-built production D.III wing uppersurfaces employed a three-tone camouflage of Venetian red, olive green, and pale green; the pattern of camouflage colors and their port or starboard directional slant varied between machines. Wing undersurfaces were pale blue. The fabric-covered rudder could be either clear doped linen or often one of the various camouflage colors. Again, this varied between machines.

National markings consisted of a white-bordered black *Eisernes Kreuz* at eight points: one at each top-wing uppersurface wing tip and each lower-wing undersurface wing tip (although some lower-wing crosses were applied directly to the pale blue undersurfaces without a white crossfield or border); one on each side of the fuselage, well aft near the horizontal stabilizer; and one on each side of the tail, overlapping the hinge line of the vertical stabilizer and the rudder. The upper-wing crosses were centered slightly inboard the interplane struts and were not quite full chord, stretching instead from the leading edge to several inches shy of the trailing edge. A black serial number such as "D.789/17" was hand-painted on either side of the vertical stabilizer ("D" represented the aircraft designation [single-engined single-seat biplane with armament]; "789" denoted it was the 40th machine of the third production batch [D.750–799/17]; and "/17" was the last two digits of the year the machine was ordered), and thus, although similar, no two numbers were exactly alike. Manufacturer and Idflieg placards were located on either side of the nose and on the leading edge of the lower wings, just outboard of the interplane struts. Finally, an Albatros company logo (a helmeted bird with wings spread in flight) adorned each side of the rudder and was applied so that both port and starboard birds faced (i.e. "flew toward") the spinner.

Ostdeutsche Albatros Werke (D.1650–1849/17; D.2362–2599/17; D.3056–3255/17; D.5022–5221/17)

OAW-built Albatros D.IIIs were finished similarly to their Johannisthal brethren – warm, straw-yellow fuselage, gray or grayish-beige metal fittings, with the wings and horizontal stabilizers/elevator finished in dark green and mauve (lilac) uppersurfaces with pale blue undersurfaces. *Eisernes Kreuz* national markings were located at the usual eight points, all of which bore a 5cm white border. Upper wing crosses were centered atop the interplane struts, and fuselage crosses were located further forward than those on the Johannisthal machines. Serial numbers were allocated to the wheel covers (which employed an oval rather than a rectangular valve access hatch) and to

Rear view of an Albatros D.III(OAW), illustrating OAW's use of mauve and dark green camouflage (light and dark colors, respectively). The color demarcations are wavy, hard-edged, and applied span-wise on the horizontal elevators. Note the wing crosses are centered on the aileron control arms.

the wing struts instead of the vertical stabilizer, and the fuselage manufacture and Idflieg placards were located on the upper longeron just below the cockpit.

Other visual OAW hallmarks include a ridge along the lower edges of the engine cowl panels, a rounded trailing edge to the rudder, the nose footstep, and what is believed to have been strips of fabric along the upper and lower longerons that covered engine ground wires routed aft.

Oesterreichische Flugzeugfabrik Allgemeine Gesellschaft (53.20–53.64; 153.01–153.281; 253.01–253.260)

Along with German manufacture, 586 Albatros D.IIIs were produced by Oeffag of Wiener-Neustadt, Austria. The machines of the first production series were numbered 53.20 to 53.64. The number "5" was the one Austria designated to Oeffag; "3" was the designation for Albatros; and the numbers right of the decimal point denoted the individual machines of the series. Since the Oeffag-built Friedrichshafen G.IIIa(Oef) was designated Series 54, Oeffag's subsequent Albatros D.III series required a prefix number, hence Series 53, 153, and 253.

Overall they employed the same semi-monocoque wooden construction of the German machines, with the spinner, cowl panels, and access hatches in bare, engine-turned metal. The wings, horizontal stabilizers, and all

D

1. ALBATROS D.III 2062/16, FLOWN BY LTN KARL SCHAEFER, JASTA 11, MARCH 1917

One of the several Albatros D.IIIs flown by 30-victory ace Karl Schaefer, this machine from the first production batch featured his usual black overpainting from mid-fuselage aft, with all factory markings and insignia untouched. This aircraft had a central radiator, wooden wing root fairings, and an airspeed anemometer mounted on the forward port interplane strut. A field-modified tube was affixed to the fuselage through which a flare gun was fired. 2062/16 was photographed on March 9, 1917 after Schaefer – while shooting down a No. 40 Sqn F.E.8 – experienced a synchronization gear malfunction and shot seven bullets through one of his Axial propeller blades. This caused extreme vibration and forced Schaefer to either throttle to idle or switch the engine off, precipitating an immediate descent and forced landing.

2. ALBATROS D.III (SERIAL NO. U/K), JASTA 11, MARCH 1917

Strikingly overpainted, this first production batch D.III has been photographed with other Jasta 11 machines and featured red-and-white striped fuselage and tail. The wings retained their factory colors but the undersurfaces of the lower wings featured red/white/red/white/ red stripes in a fashion similar to Allied invasion stripes of World War II. Interestingly, this machine employed twin radiators that were served by a single coolant pipe that led from the engine in the usual manner but branched into an inverted "U" to connect to both radiators.

3. ALBATROS D.III(OEF) 153.112, FLOWN BY OBLT FRIEDRICH NAVRATIL, FLIK 41J, APRIL 1918

Built by the Austrian company Oeffag, this machine was covered with printed fabric – apparently atop the birch skin – employing a seven-color hexagonal pattern. Note that the engine is fully housed and the wheel spokes are uncovered.

4. ALBATROS D.III (SERIAL NO. U/K), JASTA 18, FLOWN BY OBLT ERNST TURCK, OCTOBER/NOVEMBER 1917

Although at first glance this appears to be an OAW-built machine, close scrutiny of a photograph revealed that this is actually a first production batch Johannisthal machine, fitted with a replacement OAW rudder and possibly lower port wing. Clues to its true Johannisthal origin include a central radiator; lack of a nose footstep; manufacturer placards on the nose rather than by the cockpit, where OAW located them; shape of the engine cowl panels; and location of the panel lines and fuselage cross, which differed between Johannisthal and OAW. The extra louvres and hatches were in-field modifications, and note that the manufacturers' slightly different cross styles did not align on the tail.

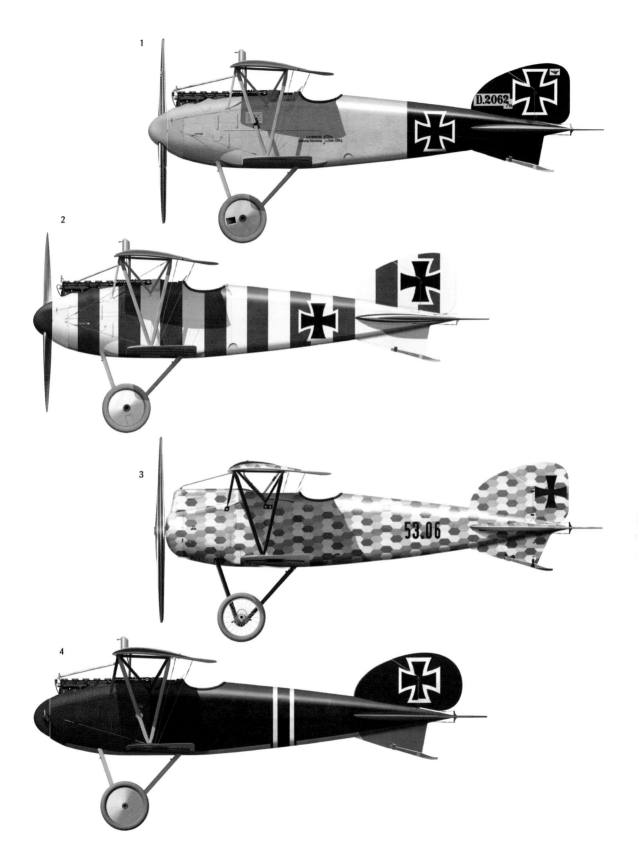

1

2

3

4

Flik 41J Hauptmann Godwin Brumowski's Albatros D.III(Oef) 153.10 well illustrates markings employed on Austrian airplanes, with heavily mottled green uppersurfaces and large black-and-white fuselage markings. Later, Brumowski painted large skulls on his fuselage, with which he has since become synonymous. The "pilot" inside the cockpit is an unidentified female.

control surfaces were covered in clear doped fabric. *Eisernes Kreuz* national markings were in the usual eight positions but were slightly different from German markings. Wing crosses were without white borders and placed fully inboard the interplane struts, while the tail cross was also borderless and positioned entirely upon the rudder. Fuselage crosses were absent on all except the very first few Series 53 machines, yet all series employed black serial numbers painted on the fuselage in large, prominent, non-serif numerals.

Staffel and Flik Finishes

The D.III's arrival coincided with the increasing use of garish Staffel and personal markings that became common by mid-1917. Initially using letters and numbers for personal identification, Staffeln realized via in-air practical experience that ostentatious markings would better serve recognition, with a secondary benefit of fostering unit and personal morale. Yet the Luftstreitkräfte had no standard to which the units adhered, which resulted in markings that varied widely from Staffel to Staffel. Some, such as Jasta 11, relied solely on color rather than fuselage drawings or geometric symbols. Their initial use of various colors soon transformed into each airplane having red fuselages and struts for the unit marking, with pilots using unique personal colors on the nose and tail for individual identification, which could be better seen when airborne. Contrastingly, Jasta 30 eschewed a standard unit marking and instead employed a hodge-podge of various personal markings, with each Albatros featuring a differently painted tail or fuselage marking. One machine had its entire fuselage painted and *also* a personalized marking. On the Eastern and Italian fronts, Oeffag machines were just as garishly painted as German airplanes, with widespread use of skulls, birds, and geometric shapes. Various airplanes were solidly overpainted, such as Brumowski's red Albatrosses, or done so with a heavily mottled application. Still others had their flying surfaces covered with swirled printed fabric, although this was a factory rather than field application.

OPERATIONAL HISTORY

The first Albatros D.IIIs arrived at the Western Front during the last days of December 1916, only three months after the first Albatros D.I had arrived in September. By the new year there were fewer than 20 D.IIIs in-country but their numbers swelled to nearly 150 by the end of February. Despite the increasing inventory the new D.IIIs did not replace the earlier Albatros D.Is and D.IIs – as both models were less than three months old, these machines could hardly be considered "old" – but instead assimilated into Staffeln complements. For example, Jasta Boelcke employed all three models concurrently.

One Staffel that rostered but a single Albatros of any kind that January was Jasta 11. Equipped with Halberstadt D.IIs and D.Vs, the unit's sole Albatros D.III arrived in mid-January when newly appointed Staffelführer Leutnant Manfred von Richthofen brought one with him when he transferred from Jasta Boelcke. This D.III featured an all-red fuselage (although it is uncertain if this machine was painted red just before Richthofen's departure from Jasta Boelcke or just after his arrival at Jasta 11) and became known as *Le petit Rouge* (The Little Red). After being credited with downing a No. 40 Squadron F.E.8 on January 23 for his 17th victory, Richthofen was aloft the following afternoon with at least one other Jasta 11 pilot, and at 12:15 attacked "the commanding plane of an enemy squadron" as its crew were taking mosaic photographs of Vimy Ridge. As both the pilot and observer of No. 25 Squadron F.E.2b 6997 were engaged in this attention-demanding task – and with their pre-arranged three-airplane escort late to arrive – Richthofen approached unseen and attacked the two-seater pusher from behind, shooting up its fuel and oil tanks, damaging the propeller, and wounding the pilot Captain Oscar Greig in the right ankle. The F.E.2's engine quit and Greig put the machine into

Albatros	D.III	D.III(OAW)	D.III(Oef), Series 53
Engine	160Ps Mercedes D.III	160Ps Mercedes D.III	185Ps Daimler
Wingspan (upper)	8.5m (27ft 11in)	8.5m (27ft 11in)	9.0m (29ft 6in)
Wingspan (lower)	8m (26ft 3in)	8m (26ft 3in)	8.73m (28ft 7in)
Chord (upper wing)	1.6m (5ft 3in)	1.6m (5ft 3in)	1.5m (4ft 11in)
Chord (lower wing)	1.6m (5ft 3in)	1.6m (5ft 3in)	1.1m (3ft 7in)
Dihedral	none	none	none upper; 1° lower
Length	7.4m (24ft 3in)	7.4m (24ft 3in)	7.4m (24ft 3in)
Height	2.95m (9ft 8in)	2.64m (8ft 8in)	2.8m (9ft 2in)
Armament	2 x IMG 08/15 7.92mm MG	2x IMG 08/15 7.92mm MG	1 or 2 M07/12 8.0mm MG
Weight (lb)			
Empty	1,530	1,484	1,530
Useful load	502	496	590
Loaded	2,032	1,980	2,120
Max speed (mph)	109	109	108
Climb to			
1,000m (3,281ft)	4 min	4 min	3 min 20 sec – 4 min 30 sec
2,000m (6,562ft)	10 min	10 min	7 min
3,000m (9,843ft)	19 min	19 min	14 min 30 sec – 19 min
4,000m (13,123ft)	30 min	30 min	–

Albatros	D.III(Oef), Series 153	D.III(Oef), Series 253
Engine	200Ps Daimler	225Ps Daimler
Wingspan (upper)	9.0m (29ft 6in)	9.0m (29ft 6in)
Wingspan (lower)	8.73m (28ft 7in)	8.73m (28ft 7in)
Chord (upper wing)	1.5m (4ft 11in)	1.5m (4ft 11in)
Chord (lower wing)	1.1m (3ft 7in)	1.1m (3ft 7in)
Dihedral	none upper; 1° lower	none upper; 1° lower
Length	7.35m (24ft 3in)	7.25m (23ft 9.5in)
Height	2.80m (9ft 2in)	2.80m (9ft 2in)
Armament	8.0mm MG	8.0mm MG
Weight (lb)		
Empty	1,560	1,578
Useful load	600	637
Loaded	2,160	2,215
Max speed (mph)	116	125
Climb to		
1,000m (3,281ft)	2 min 35 sec	2 min 15 sec
2,000m (6,562ft)	6 min 34 sec	5 min 15 sec
3,000m (9,843ft)	11 min 21 sec	9 min 15 sec
4,000m (13,123ft)	18 min 16 sec	14 min 15 sec
5,000m (16,404ft)	31 min 42 sec	20 min 15 sec

a spiral glide to evade further attack which, as was Richthofen's modus operandi, he did, despite the engineless predicament of his foe. Observer Leutnant John MacLennan stated, "each time [Richthofen attacked] from below and behind, in which position we were unable to return fire." Greig reported seeing, "… several tracer bullets pass through the instrument board between me and my observer," but neither man was hit again. The F.E.2 was not damaged enough to prevent Greig from making a successful dead-stick landing between Vimy and Fresnoy, and he and MacLennan set fire to their airplane before being taken prisoner.

However, during these events the new Albatros D.III sesquiplane "wing failure syndrome" reared its ugly head when one of Richthofen's lower wings failed structurally, forcing him to make an immediate precautionary landing prior to further in-air failure and/or loss of control. In a personal letter Richthofen later recalled, "… one of my wings broke in two during the air battle at three-hundred-meter altitude. It was only through a miracle that I reached the ground without going kaput." But while it is clear that Richthofen's Albatros D.III suffered structural wing failure and a subsequent forced landing, the specifics regarding what occurred immediately afterward are somewhat cloudy. Richthofen's autobiography, *Der rote Kampfflieger*, recounts this victory but there are several discrepancies between that account, his combat report, and other reports/recollections of the combatants. His autobiography states that after damaging the F.E.2, Richthofen believed the crew had been wounded and felt "deep compassion for my opponent and decided not to send him plunging down." He witnessed the F.E.2 eventually burst into flames before reaching the ground and then experienced "at about five-hundred-meter altitude, a malfunction in my machine [i.e. wing failure] during a normal glide [that] forced me to land before making another turn." He described landing his D.III amongst some barbed wire near the downed F.E.2, overturning, speaking with Greig and MacLennan personally ("I enjoyed talking with them") about this "careless" landing, and then learning from them that his red D.III was known as *Le petit Rouge*. Richthofen's combat report (written immediately after the event and not dictated some four months later, as was his autobiography) corroborates that Greig and MacLennan set fire to the F.E.2 themselves *after* landing and that Richthofen's Albatros D.III wing "cracked" at 300 meters, an altitude which dovetails with what Richthofen wrote in a personal letter to his mother three days later, on January 27. His combat report also states, "according to the English inmates my red painted plane was not unknown to them, as when being asked who had brought them down they answered: 'Le petit Rouge.'"

However, Floyd Gibbons' postwar interview (pre-1927) with MacLennan indicates the observer never spoke with Richthofen: "As regards the red machine, we had previously seen it, but we did not know who it was. I am glad to hear that he had to land, as I did not know this." Unless MacLennan is lying, it is almost without question that had Richthofen overturned when landing and subsequently discussed that event with his foes, they would have retained the memory of speaking with the man who less than ten years before had just shot them down and then crash-landed nearby. Richthofen's combat report agrees that the Englishmen knew of his red plane but it does not state specifically he gleaned this knowledge firsthand via personal conversation. This suggests Richthofen learned of the name *Le petit Rouge* either through conversations with the soldiers who had captured and spoken with Greig and MacLennan and then relayed the information to Richthofen (perhaps if he drove to the landing site personally to scavenge the wreckage later for souvenirs; photographs show that although the airplane burned, 6997's engine manufacturer placard and rudder fabric were present amongst his collected war trophies), or by similar secondhand means. Based on Richthofen's combat report, letter to his mother, and MacLennan's recollection, the entire post-victory events as recounted in *Der rote Kampfflieger*, including any nearby

Classic photograph of Jasta 11 next to Richthofen's iconic D.III *"Le petit Rouge"* (Richthofen in the cockpit), taken at Roucourt during the glory days of "Bloody April," April 20–25, 1917. Yet in just over two months, Allmenröder, Festner, and Schaefer (first, third, and fourth from left, respectively) would be dead; Richthofen, Wolff, and Lothar von Richthofen (cockpit, fifth from left, sitting in front) would be wounded; Simon (second from right) taken prisoner; and Brauneck (far right) would have but weeks to live.

overturned landing, were likely fabricated as autobiographical embellishment.

The Albatros D.III spate of wing failures and subsequent groundings had a silver lining of sorts: they came in winter when air combat had slowed. Slowed, but not stopped: sorties were still flown, victories and losses were still had, and as the year progressed more Jagdstaffeln were created and employed at the front. Thus, the pace naturally grew and intensified. Future Orden Pour le Mérite winners, such as Ernst Udet, Werner Voss, Adolf von Tutschek, Lothar von Richthofen, Otto Bernert, Kurt Wolff, Rudolf Berthold, and Karl Schaefer were scoring victories in their new D.IIIs. In March, fully aware of a pending Allied spring offensive, Germany initiated a preparatory strategic withdrawal to consolidate and better defend its lines, the Siegfriedstellung or "Hindenburg Line." Allied strategic need for information was paramount and forced the French and British to sortie continual reconnaissance two-seater flights into German territory – where along with the D.II the new Albatros D.III awaited to exact a terrible tactical toll.

Despite the persistent and archaic Waldo-Pepper-tainted belief that most World War I aerial combat was fighter-versus-fighter-silk-scarf-chivalry, in reality the Jagdstaffeln primarily hunted two-seater observation airplanes, although of course they fought all comers. With two-seaters continually sent aloft to gather information for the planned French attack on the Chemin des Dames on April 16 and the French-requested British diversionary attack on Arras on April 9, the Germans inflicted large losses upon their foes, despite having fewer than 50 fighters to sortie at certain points along the front.

A case in point was Jasta 11 pilot Leutnant Lothar von Richthofen. Two and a half years younger than his brother and Jasta 11 Staffelführer Manfred, Lothar had begun the war in cavalry unit Dragoner-Regiment Nr 4 and fought in Belgium, France, and on the Eastern Front. In summer 1915 he trained as an aerial observer and then flew reconnaissance and bombing sorties with Kampfstaffel 23. Lothar enjoyed bombing, as had his brother, writing after the war: "This work as bomber crewman was very satisfying. We were scarcely back from our first flight when our crate was again loaded with bombs and filled with fuel. Meanwhile, we sat in the officers' mess and drank to work up new courage. This went on three or four times a night." Eventually Lothar learned to fly between his observer sorties and soloed for the first time on December 26, 1916. Upon passing the required flight exams, Manfred's influence as Staffelführer and 25-victory ace enabled Lothar to bypass the usual route of two-seater pilot and *Jastaschule* and instead transfer directly into Jasta 11 on March 10. There he received personal tutelage from Manfred, as had Manfred from Oswald Boelcke. (See Osprey's *Air Vanguard 5, Albatros D.I –D.II.*) Two weeks later, Lothar was flying an Albatros D.III with Karl Schaefer, Kurt Wolff, Karl Allmenröder, and Eddy Lübbert – all much more experienced pilots

Lothar von Richthofen in the cockpit of a first production-batch D.III. Items of interest include apparent repair patches on the wings and fuselage; nonstandard windscreen; padding on the ladder; central radiator; and round footstep. Taken at Roucourt, *c.* late April, 1917.

than him, and all but Lübbert future Orden Pour le Mérite winners – and damaged a "Bristol." Four days later, on March 28, he attacked No. 25 Squadron F.E.2b 7715, wounding the pilot and forcing him to land for his first victory. Lothar did not score again until after the battle of Arras had begun, when on April 11 he shot down No. 28 Squadron Bristol F.2a A3323 and No. 59 Squadron R.E.8 A4190. By month's end he had downed another 13 airplanes, and by May 13 had amassed 24 credited victories in the mere 44 days since his first victory as a combat pilot. Among these and most famous was No. 56 Squadron 44-victory ace and RFC luminary Captain Albert Ball, although the provenance of this victory is questionable (Lothar claimed a Sopwith Triplane, but Ball flew an S.E.5 biplane), controversial, and, in retrospect, unlikely. However, Ball's demise remains amongst Lothar's officially credited victories.

As was the D.III a boon for the novice, so it was for the experienced. With two-seater RFC reconnaissance machines crossing the lines regularly, Staffel pilots who had been hamstrung cither by poor weather or a lack of experience or inferior airplanes now enjoyed a confluence of circumstances that saw the dissipation of these hindrances, enabling them to begin amassing unprecedented victory tallies.

Such was the case with Jasta 11's Ltn Kurt Wolff. Born on February 6, 1895 in Greifswald, Wolff began the war with Eisenbahn Regiment Nr 4 (Railway Regiment No. 4) and transferred into the Fliegertruppen in July 1916. After learning to fly he served with various two-seater units until posting to Jasta 11 in October 1916. There he continued to gain stick and rudder experience flying Halberstadt machines, but Wolff – nay, the entire Staffel – scored no victories that year. Jasta 11's first victory came with newly appointed Staffelführer Richthofen's 17th victory on January 23, but it was not until March 6 that Wolff first scored, shooting down a No. 16 Squadron B.E.2d while flying a machine described by Eddy Lübbert as "plum purple." Wolff scored steadily throughout March, shooting down five airplanes (three two-seaters and two single-seaters). However, the following month – hence known infamously as "Bloody April" – Wolff was credited with shooting down 22 airplanes, a one-month total that bested all other pilots in Jasta 11, as well as the entire Luftstreitkräfte. Moreover, Wolff's streak was the largest one-month total amassed by a German pilot during the entire war. This tally included 14 two-seaters, eight single-seaters, and a single day during which he shot down four airplanes. Six days later he received a new 600-series Albatros D.III, 632/17, which is believed to have had its fuselage painted all-red (rather than plum purple) to adhere to the red unit markings adopted by Jasta 11 at this time. Regarding the use of red, Lothar von Richthofen wrote:

It became known all over that the English had put a price on my brother's head [this was an untrue rumour that Jasta 11 pilots believed]. Every flier over there knew him, for at the time he alone flew a red aeroplane. For that reason we wanted to paint every aeroplane in our squadron, and we pleaded with my brother not to be so conspicuous. The request was granted, for through our many victories we had shown ourselves worthy of the color. The color red signified a certain arrogance. Everyone knew that. It attracted attention … My brother's crate was glaring red [*Le petit Rouge*]. The rest of us each had his own special mark painted in other colors. In the air one cannot see another flier's face, so we chose these colors as recognition insignia. For example, Schäfer had the elevator, rudder, and rear part of the fuselage in black, Allmenröder had the same in white, Wolff had green, and I had yellow.

Kurt Wolff's 632/17, before and after. Top view shows the brand-new, gleaming machine in factory markings. Bottom view shows Wolff next to the same airplane, the fuselage of which is now entirely overpainted – mostly red, with some portions painted green for Wolff's personal identification. Although there is a tantalizingly possible vertical color demarcation just aft of the footstep, how much green was used and where has yet to be determined.

It is uncertain exactly how much green Wolff's D.III possessed. Lothar described Allmenröder's Albatros as "the same" as Schaefer's, with his personal color painted on the elevator, rudder, and rear part of the fuselage, yet photographs show not just the control surfaces but the entire empennage of Schaefer's Albatrosses (he had at least two different D.IIIs painted similarly) so painted. However, photographs also reveal Allmenröder's 629/17 was not painted "the same" as Schaefer's but had only the elevator overpainted in his personal color white, not the entire empennage. Photos of Wolff's 632/17 offer

E **THREE ACES**

On September 2, 1917, Jasta 2 ace Werner Voss flew to LaBrayelle airfield to visit his former comrade Manfred von Richthofen, now Staffelführer of Jasta 11. After a "long and delightful conversation" Voss took off for his return journey, with Richthofen accompanying. Flying a "roundabout way over the Front," the pair happened upon a third Albatros D.III flown by Richthofen's brother Lothar, who had become separated from his flight during an earlier sortie. This chance meeting is the only known sortie involving these three men, who eventually accounted for 168 credited victories between them.

Soon they spotted several No. 43 Squadron Sopwith Strutters flying over British territory. To Richthofen they seemed hesitant to engage in battle (he later opined that it was because he had been recognized by the color of his red Albatros) but soon he was involved with a Strutter who "knew what it was all about and was a very good shot. I found that out very well, to my sorrow." After drifting with the wind into German territory, eventually the Strutter dived into the thin undercast to disengage but Richthofen followed and shot its fuel tanks, causing the Strutter to emit a "white vapor of fuel" behind it. The damaged fuel tank lost pressure and led to engine failure, forcing the aircraft to glide to a successful dead-stick landing for Richthofen's 33rd victory. Yet his combat report claims events were not so smooth and that the Strutter continued firing at him, hitting his Albatros "very severely." This got Richthofen's dander up enough to prosecute a punitive post-landing strafing attack against the downed Strutter. Although Richthofen believed this attack had killed one of the Strutter's crewmen, there were no further injuries.

no help, as definitive color demarcations cannot be seen. It is likely that some part of its empennage was green, as perhaps was its spinner and front cowl panels, such as on other Jasta 11 machines, but the exact manner of application is yet to be determined.

In any regard, Wolff attained 29 credited victories while flying an Albatros with Jasta 11. On May 4 he was awarded the Orden Pour le Mérite and two days later appointed as Jasta 29 Staffelführer. Thence his victory pace slowed, however, and he shot down only one airplane in May (a French SPAD from Escadrille N.37) and one in June (No. 60 Squadron Nieuport 23). His 33rd and final victory was attained on July 7 when he shot down a No. 1 Naval Squadron Sopwith Triplane. By then Wolff had been transferred into Jasta 11 as Staffelführer after Allmenröder – who had been appointed Staffelführer when Richthofen was selected to lead newly formed Jagdgeschwader Nr 1 – was shot down and killed on June 27, after downing 21 airplanes since May 7 for 30 total credited victories. Yet just over one week later on July 11 Wolff was shot in the left wrist and forced to convalesce for several weeks. Upon his return to flight status he began flying Fokker F.I 102/17, a preproduction triplane sent to the front for Richthofen's combat evaluation that Wolff was allowed to fly in Richthofen's absence during leave. It was in this machine that Wolff was shot down and killed on September 15, 1917.

Meanwhile, Jasta Boelcke was another breeding ground for stellar, Pour le Mérite-bound fighter pilots amassing large victory tallies while flying Albatros D.IIIs. One of the most famous – although he is known more for the events of his death than those of his life – was Leutnant Werner Voss. Born on April 13, 1897 in Krefeld, Germany, Voss began World War I as a member of the Westfälisches Husaren-Regiment Nr 11 but was granted transfer into the Fliegertruppe a year later. After learning to fly he spent a month in Cologne as a flight instructor before posting to Kampfstaffel (Kasta) 20 of Kampfgeschwader Nr IV, flying reconnaissance and bombing sorties around Verdun. In the summer of 1916 he was commissioned as a *Leutnant der Reserve* and assigned to Jasta 2 on November 21, 1916. There it is unclear whether Voss was first assigned an Albatros D.I or D.II – the Staffel employed both types during that autumn – but with one or the other model Voss shot down his first airplanes less than a week later, when he downed a Nieuport 17 and a DH.2. Scoring a double on the day of his inaugural air-combat success was a portent of things to come. Although he only shot down one more airplane in 1916, a B.E.2d on December 21, and went without success in January, Voss scored eight victories in February: four DH.2s and four B.E.2s. Again, the model of Albatros flown during these victories is uncertain. At this point the new D.III had arrived at Jasta 2, but its quick grounding undoubtedly saw the retention and use of the D.II and early D.Is. But it is certain Voss was flying an early-production D.III shortly thereafter, as were the rest of the Staffel, with Voss's machine personally decorated with heart, swastika, and laurel wreath markings.

Conflict exists regarding this famous Albatros D.III. Various photographs show this airplane with and without stripes on the upper wings, and with and without a third heart on the top of the fuselage, just aft of the cockpit (a location known as the "turtledeck," a term associated more with Fokker machines but descriptive for many airplanes). Other photographs show the airplane with a central and then an

Manfred von Richthofen near Werner Voss's famous Albatros D.III, in a photograph taken in June, 1917. Close inspection beneath the point of the heart reveals a round footstep, a feature of first production-batch machines.

offset radiator, indicating Voss either had two similarly painted machines or that the same machine was photographed at different stages of markings, at some point during which its upper wings were replaced.

Belief in two different machines is born from photos of Voss painting the port fuselage heart on a D.III that had a round footstep and central radiator. Other photos of this machine in the same location reveal it had no stripes on the wings and no heart on the turtledeck, and the absence of these markings is also seen in photos taken when Voss was on leave in April 1916, after winning the Orden Pour le Mérite. The presence of a central radiator indicates this D.III was a first production-batch machine prior to 2252/16, and the rounded footstep indicates it was built prior to 2108/16. However, photographs taken a few months later in June show an offset radiator, a turtledeck heart, and stripes on the upper wings. The offset radiator and louvres visible on the annular nose cowl fostered a belief that this was actually a different D.III than the one photographed in April, since radiator relocation came after the switch from rounded to rectangular footsteps, and louvres were thought to be a feature of the third production batch (750-series) of D.IIIs. Because of this, Voss's machine was believed to have been a 750-series machine and thus must have had a rectangular footstep, despite it not being seen in photographs. However, continued research indicates cowl louvres were *not* a production feature of the 750-series but actually a Jasta Boelcke field modification. Several of their D.IIIs featured these louvres, including machines from the first production batch that have central radiators and round footsteps. In fact, other than those machines in Jasta B, most Albatros D.IIIs – 750-series or otherwise – do not have such louvres; that is, they were not an absolute hallmark of the 750-series, or any other series. Therefore, that Voss's airplane had these louvres and offset radiator does *not* mean his footstep must have been square and the machine must have been a 750-series – that is, a different machine than the earlier machine with the central radiator. Further proof against a 750-series was gleaned after study of high-resolution digital scans revealed Voss's D.III with the offset radiator and turtledeck heart *did* have a round footstep – a feature definitely not found on 750-series machines – and the machine lacked the rectangular nose footstep that *is* a hallmark of the 750-series (as well as 600-series and OAW) machines. Consequently, the Albatros D.III with the heart/swastika/wreath in all photographs was *not* a 600- or 750-series Albatros D.III but rather a first production-batch machine.

Additionally, several layered-comparisons have been made between high-resolution scans of the wreaths photographed in April and June 1917. The wreaths on the April machine with the central radiator and no turtledeck heart match the wreaths on the June machine with the turtledeck heart and offset radiator, right down to the scalloped edges of the leaves (a detail too small to be discerned in most published photos) and the number of leaves on each side of the wreaths. In both sets of April and June photographs the right sides of the starboard wreaths (i.e. right of the center bow) had 16 leaves and the left sides had 15, for 31 total. On the port wreaths, the right sides had 14 leaves

Voss's machine with and without the turtledeck heart, shown in photographs taken months apart. Even casual observation here reveals identical wreaths, bows, and placement of each. Similarly, each photo shows smudges above and below the left portions of the fuselage cross, and the same wavy unevenness of the topmost swastika border.

51

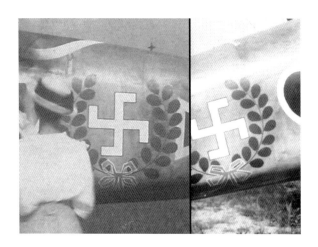

Voss's airplane, in photos taken in April (right, to starboard, without turtledeck heart) and June (left, to port, with turtledeck heart). Note both views show some sort of seam repair on the turtledeck forward of the swastika. No markings match, which demonstrates that any stencil used was not of the entire wreath but of a single leaf; that is, the stencil was used numerous times to place each leaf by hand. For this placement to match so precisely in the previous photograph is at best extremely unlikely if on two different machines painted months apart.

and the left sides had 15 leaves, for 29 total. Voss's mechanic recalled that after he painted the white swastika it "looked rather bare" so he "added a laurel wreath using a cardboard stencil as a guide to marking the leaves." It has been presumed the stencil was used to create the *entire* wreath, but "guide to marking the leaves" suggests the stencil was not the entire wreath but a single leaf to be used over and over to paint so many leaves. High resolution layered-comparison supports this, for when the starboard wreath from an April photograph is compared with/superimposed over the wreath from the port side of the same machine they do not match, neither in the number of leaves (31 versus 29) nor in their arrangement and placement. Neither does a wreath taken from the starboard side of the D.III photographed in April match with the port wreath of the D.III photographed in June. If the entire wreaths were created using one complete stencil, then why is there a different number of leaves on each side of the same airplane, and why do the wreaths not match? Additionally, the port and starboard bows of the airplanes photographed with a central and offset radiator match each other, but the bows on the port and starboard sides of the airplane with the same radiator do not. If a complete stencil was used, then these features ought to be virtually identical in every photograph. That they are not supports the statement of Voss's mechanic that a single leaf stencil was used, ostensibly free-handedly, to create the wreaths which, when the starboard or port wreaths on the machine photographed in April are compared with their starboard or port counterparts in the June photographs, match in number of leaves and locations of same.

It is not far-fetched to speculate that without a complete wreath stencil, even Michelangelo could not replicate an exact leaf pattern on two different machines, right down to their angular orientation, spacing from each other, distance from panel lines, and extent markings on the machine, and so on. Perhaps if one measured or drew guidelines one could attain identical and precisely oriented leaves between two separate machines, but there was no need for such nth-degree precision in Voss's situation.

Although it is reasonably certain that Voss's photographed D.IIIs were the same machine, why would it have two different radiator locations? Whether the radiator was relocated or the entire wing was replaced is unclear, as are the associated reasons for either. One possibility is that this resulted from a radiator change when warmer weather led to overheating, but that is just one of a myriad of possibilities and itself invites a host of more, at this time, unanswerable questions.

When Voss's D.III was painted has also been debated. However, the hangar visible in the background of the photograph of Voss painting his D.III is also seen in the background of the image of the airplane with finished markings (heart/swastika/wreath, but no turtledeck heart), and it is the same hangar seen in the background of a photograph of Jasta B Ltn Hermann Frommherz's "*Blau Maus*" Albatros D.III. Measured and compared board-for-board between the Voss and Frommherz photographs, the buildings match identically. Since Frommherz's only Albatros D.III Staffel was Jasta B, and he served with that unit at Proville, and the hangar in the Frommherz photograph matches a

hangar in an aerial shot of Proville, Voss's plane must have been painted at Proville; that is, *before* he went to Jasta 5, and not after as has been claimed – which makes sense, since Voss's machine was photographed with heart/swastika/wreath in April. Further corroborating evidence is the dark stripe on Voss's fuselage, just ahead of the junction with the leading edge of the horizontal stabilizers. Such a stripe in that location was present on several Jasta B D.IIIs, but absent on Jasta 5 D.IIIs. Yet where and when the wing stripes and turtledeck heart were applied is uncertain. As discussed, they were not present in the photos taken in April, but they are present in June. Voss went to Jasta 5 in late May so it is possible, even likely, the wing stripes were applied there, since such markings were common with Jasta 5 machines. Or, they could have been already applied to any replacement wings installed on Voss's machine. The turtledeck heart has no such Staffel association and thus its date of application is harder to theorize, but it is possible it could have been painted while Voss was with Jasta 5. Certainly it was in place by June, and Voss remained with the Staffel until June 10.

A less iconic Jasta B pilot was Ltn Fritz Otto Bernert. Born in the Upper Silesia region of Germany on March 6, 1893, Bernert had joined the 173rd Infantry Regiment and was wounded several times early in the war. The last of these wounds is said to have been inflicted when he was bayonetted in the left arm, severing a nerve and rendering the limb "nearly useless," causing Bernert's transfer to the Fliegertruppe. There he flew as an observer for FFA 27 (Feldflieger Abteilung, or "Field Flying Company") and FFA 71 before learning to fly and subsequently fighting with Kek Vaux (*Kampfeinsitzer-Kommando* Vaux) and Jasta 4, amassing seven victories before joining Jasta B in February 1917. Although his two victories in March lagged behind Voss's 11 victories, Bernert caught his stride during Bloody April and was credited with 15 victories. Incredibly, five came on a single day, when on April 24 – the day after he was awarded the Orden Pour le Mérite – he claimed three B.E.2s,

Location where Voss's machine was first painted, at Proville aerodrome, when Voss flew there with Jasta Boelcke. Features on the vertical boards seen in the top photo of Voss's machine precisely match those in the bottom right photograph of Jasta B Leutnant Hermann Frommherz's D.III. Construction features at the left side of the hangar match as well and correspond with an aerial view of Proville.

Jasta Boelcke's Otto Bernert smiles broadly and waves enthusiastically with his "bad" arm in photographic stills taken from a Fokker cine-film. Ostensibly jovial and without any visible distress or hindrance of motion, this footage confirms the exaggeration of Bernert's "nearly useless" left arm.

one Sopwith 1½ Strutter, and a DH.4. His final victory for the month brought his total victory tally to 24.

It has been noted that Bernert's achievements were even more extraordinary in light of his "nearly useless" left arm. But it did not take two arms to fly an Albatros; the left hand mainly controlled the throttle lever on the control column, and could assist in high-G maneuvers if necessary, but shooting down mostly balloons and two-seater reconnaissance airplanes did not require much high-G maneuvering. In any case, a cine-film shot by Anthony Fokker suggests that too much of a meal has been made of Bernert's "nearly useless" arm, for he is shown smiling broadly and waving with his left arm animatedly for several seconds. Quite obviously he is without pain and enjoyed much more freedom of motion of his arm than would ever be required in the cockpit of an Albatros D.III.

In any event, Bernert left Jasta Boelcke to become Staffelführer of Jasta 6, with whom he scored three more victories until he was injured when landing long, suffering among other things a broken jaw. Returning to Jasta Boelcke as Staffelführer in June, he scored no further victories and ultimately worked with the Inspector of the Flying Service after he posted out of Jasta Boelcke for "war weariness" (as detailed in Osprey's *Aviation Elite Units 26: Jagdstaffel 2 'Boelcke'*). Thereafter free from combat he likely would have survived the war if not for contracting influenza during the worldwide "Spanish flu" pandemic of 1918. Although it is claimed Bernert's "war weary" condition attributed to his illness by making him unable to fight the infection, in actual fact the Spanish flu predominantly killed previously healthy young adults via a "cytokine storm," which is an overreaction of the body's immune system. Individuals with weaker immune systems died less often than those with healthy immune systems. In any event, Bernert died as a result of contracting this influenza – pneumonia was the primary cause of mortality for most – on October 18, 1918.

One Albatros D.III with which the Royal Flying Corps became familiar was Jasta 11 Leutnant Georg Simon's 2015/16. As were many Jasta 11 machines, Simon's fuselage was entirely overpainted red with a 3ft-wide green band ("composed of common Brunswick green and white") just aft of the cockpit. Flying this machine from Jasta 11's Roucourt aerodrome on June 4, the single-victory Simon was shot down in the early evening by a No. 29 Squadron Nieuport 17. Landing the machine intact, Simon was taken prisoner and 2015/16 was seized as a war trophy. Assigned the captured "G" number G.42, it was test flown by several RFC pilots who recorded their impressions of its flight characteristics. No. 56 Squadron pilot Cecil Lewis wrote:

I don't know what it [the fuselage] was made of, but it gave the impression of *papier maché*. However; being rounded out like a fish, it was far more roomy and the whole machine seemed larger because of this cavernous cockpit. The engine, water-cooled, had a neat radiator in the centre-section, but it was big and heavy. In fact the Germanic temperament showed up all along. The machine was sluggish, strong, reliable and determined. It had none of the feeling of lightness and grace that our aircraft had. Of course, every aeroplane has its own characteristics and very few pilots could take over the controls of a strange type and really measure up its capabilities in an hour or so. So it is probable we never really stretched it; but I am certain of one thing – to throw an Albatros around in the air was hard work and it would have made you sweat in a dogfight.

No. 66 Sopwith Pup pilot Sir Patrick Gordon Taylor also flew Simon's Albatros and wrote about the experience in his 1968 memoir *Sopwith Scout 7309*. He found the view from the cockpit to be excellent and virtually without blind spots, and considered the sound of the Mercedes engine to be "savage and impressive" compared to the Pup's LeRhone engine. Taylor then took off:

The machine moved away with a bellowing roar and began to gather speed. It seemed to run quite a distance before it showed any inclination to leave the ground... A little back pressure on the stick and the Albatros was airborne, and away. I held the machine in a steady climb to 1,000 feet, then applied the controls to a left-hand turn. Laterally it was quite light, but when I steepened the turn and tried to pull the machine around with the elevator it seemed very heavy, putting up a resistance to the turn. I could see why the Albatros pilots kept out of the close duelling turns.

Taylor then reapplied full-throttle to experiment with climbs and was unhappy to see that although the aircraft didn't climb with the "lift-like action of a slow and lightly loaded aircraft," it did surge forward "very convincingly." At high angles of climb it hung on the prop. However, when diving the machine, he experienced the Albatros's strong points:

Then I let the nose go down. The speed built up steadily, giving me the impression that the heavy Albatros would go on accelerating indefinitely, drawn on by the power of its engine, unopposed by the beautiful, streamlined fuselage. It was fast, and that was obvious. As far as I could judge, its maximum speed was about 125 mph; perhaps a little more.

I brought the machine in; landed, and taxied to the hangars... Its personality was utterly different from our own airy Sopwith Scout. Ours was, in some indefinable way, a sporting weapon, with a slightly smiling light-hearted personality; a machine which did not identify itself readily with the slaughter of war. But this Hun was a war machine, a weapon of ruthless efficiency...

My thoughts, as I got out of the Albatros's cockpit, can be similarly expressed, "Give me this aeroplane to fight the war. Let me keep the Sopwith Scout to enjoy myself in the air when the war is won."

Note that each of these accounts compares the Albatros D.III with much more agile British machines, such as the Sopwith Pup. These comparisons have somewhat fostered a misbelief that the Albatros D.III was "doggy" compared with the Albatros D.I and D.II; the same misbelief is also tagged to the Albatros D.V and D.Va. Compared with such a light and nimble machine as the Pup, the Albatros D.III *was* heavier on the controls, was *not* as nimble, and *was* more physically demanding during combat maneuvers, but such comparisons should not be misinterpreted as an indication that Albatros D's performance had declined since the D.I. Incidentally, note that Taylor wrote of diving G.42 – a first production-batch machine which ostensibly had reinforced wings – without consequence.

Back in Johannisthal, the production of the Albatros D.III concluded by spring 1917 and focus shifted to the manufacture of yet another model of Albatros, the D.V. This was not the end of the D.III, as production began anew at the OAW facilities in Schneidemühl, with their first batch of 200 fighters ordered on April 23, 1917. Two D.III(OAW)s underwent testing in June. In all cases the wings passed load tests "without any significant deformation," although the rear fuselage frame failed at 73 percent and required reinforcement. A June 9 test report regarding "a biplane of the Ostdeutsche Albatros Werke, Schneidemühl" with a 160Ps engine referred to some 40 areas of improvement or refinement, from "some of the turnbuckles were screwed together too tightly" to "the elevator cables chafe in several places." These concerns must have been addressed satisfactorily because production of the D.III(OAW) ran parallel with that of the Johannisthal D.V into late 1917. However, the D.III(OAW) avoided the lower-wing structural difficulties that had plagued the older D.III – and, as it turned out, the new D.V. An Idflieg report in July stated, "The Albatros D.III is more robustly constructed than the D.V. The D.V is merely regarded as a lightened D.III. The performance of both is equal. The D.V will not be manufactured further, only the D.III[(OAW)]." Indeed, D.V production ceased while another 140 D.III(OAW)s were ordered in August.

Meanwhile, on the Italian Front that summer, Albatros D.II(Oef) and D.III(Oef) machines were trickling into Austro-Hungarian LFT inventories. One pilot with prior Albatros experience gleaned from firsthand study of German fighter combat techniques on the Western Front was Flik 41/J Commanding

F **BALLOON-BUSTING**

Although embroiled in skirmishes with other aircraft, some fighter pilots had a penchant for attacking observation balloons. Situated near the lines, these balloons were filled with hydrogen gas and floated hundreds of feet above the earth, tethered stationary by steel cables. The observers manning the balloons used binoculars and cameras to monitor enemy activities across the lines, namely troop and vehicular movement, and the location of artillery. This information could then be relayed to the ground telephonically via two-way communication cables.

The perils were many. While threatened by ground fire and attacking aircraft, balloons were also at the mercy of the weather and could be – and were – hit by lightning. One observer wrote, "...the view was mostly bad. The autumn storms drove the balloons here and there; whoever was not 'seaworthy' had a hard life." For defense, balloons were usually well covered by ground-based anti-aircraft weapons, and crews aloft were dissuaded from exchanging gunfire with attacking airplanes. Instead, they were equipped with static-line parachutes and bailed out of their baskets at the first sign of trouble. Normally they were able to drift clear of the burning remains of a falling balloon, since it was still tethered.

Some pilots ignored balloons (Manfred von Richthofen never shot one down and is not known to have ever attacked one) while others became quite proficient, such as Germany's third-highest scoring ace Oblt Erich Löwenhardt, whose first of 54 credited victories was a balloon shot down on March 24, 1917. Eventually, eight of his first 14 credited victories would be balloons. Depicted here is his fourth balloon victory, when on September 9, 1917 Löwenhardt – believed to be flying an Albatros D.III(OAW) at the time – shot down a balloon near Alveringhen, Belgium. Detailed information on the exact manner of victory is lacking, but the illustration is a good example of the fiery allure of a balloon victory.

Jasta 11 pilot Leutnant Georg Simon flew Albatros D.III 2015/16 when he was shot down on June 4 ,1917. Landing intact, Simon was taken prisoner and his green-banded red D.III was captured and given the number G.42. It is shown here in British hands post-capture, with a tricolored tail and RFC markings covering the original German markings.

Officer Hauptmann Godwin Brumowski. Born on July 26, 1889 in Wadowice, Galicia (today, Poland), Brumowski attended the Technical Military Academy in Mödling, and after graduating on August 18, 1910 he served with Austro-Hungarian Field Artillery Regiment No. 29. In July 1915 he was assigned as an observer with Flik 1 and on April 12, 1916 participated in a bombing attack on a Russian military review during a visit by Tsar Nicholas II, during which Brumowski was credited with shooting down two Morane-Saulnier Parasols for his first two victories. Learning to fly in the months afterwards, Brumowski amassed 16 victories flying airplanes such as the Hansa-Brandenburg D.I (KD), and a stint with German Jasta 24 provided practical experience flying Johannisthal-built Albatros D.IIs. Leading Flik 41/J aloft on August 19, 1917, Brumowski shot down an Italian Caudron two-seater for his first victory flying an Albatros D.III(Oef). He shot down several airplanes and balloons with Series 153 D.III(Oef)s, and soon adorned his Albatrosses by completely overpainting them red, with large white skulls on the fuselage sides.

The robustness of Oeffag construction was demonstrated via one of Brumowski's machines, when on February 1, 1918 he fought eight enemy fighters and endured at least 26 hits to his machine, some of which ignited the upper-wing fuel tank that caused the burning and loss of several square yards of fabric on his upper and lower starboard wings. Despite the severity of this damage Brumowski was unwounded and was able to land successfully. Three days later, while escorting reconnaissance airplanes in his red D.III(Oef) 153.52, Brumowski again fought several enemy fighters, until at 3,000 meters (9,800 feet) the leading edge of his lower port wing broke and took much of the fabric with it, shortly before the same happened to the starboard wing, including loss of its main spar.

Austro-Hungarian ace Godwin Brumowski's destroyed Albatros D.III(Oef) 153.52 after his combat and subsequent crash landing on February 4, 1918. The de-gloved lower-wing fabric and broken spar are clearly evident. The machine is painted in his usual red, although this time with lighter swirls, and as always a large skull adorns the fuselage.

A majestic shot of a Flik 22 Albatros D.III(Oef) flying at 3,000 meters near some cumulus clouds. Many typical Austro-Hungarian Albatros markings are evident, including mid-wing crosses, rudder cross, metal wing root fairings, redesigned rounded nose sans spinner, and quite discernible personal markings.

Although reminiscent of early German-built D.III wing failures, this incident appears to have been caused by enemy fire or aggressive high-G evasive action. In any event, Brumowski again managed to extricate himself from the fight and reach the ground safely, albeit turning over landing. He was unwounded but his D.III(Oef) was destroyed.

Back on the Western Front, frustrations were brewing amongst the German pilots regarding the Albatros D.III. In early spring the Germans had held a tactical advantage hunting various two-seater reconnaissance airplanes escorted by either other two-seaters or outdated single-seat DH.2 and F.E.8 pushers. But by the arrival of the D.III(OAW) in summer, the Germans were facing new British and French machines in ever increasing numbers. Instead of fighting pushers, the Albatrosses were facing such offensive threats as the SPAD VII, S.E.5 and 5a, Sopwith Pup, Sopwith Triplane, Bristol F.2a/b, and the famous Sopwith Camel. The RFC two-seaters were improving as well, at least compared with the venerable B.E.2 that was finally retired from front-line service. The R.E.8 and Armstrong Whitworth F.K.8 were hardly invulnerable, albeit improvements over the B.E.2s, and the AMC DH.4 enjoyed speed and a good measure of altitude for defense. Most troubling was the pusher F.E.2d, which featured a 250hp engine that gave it a significant increase in climb rate and ceiling over the 120hp F.E.2b and enabled the "d" model to carry a third Lewis machine gun that was fixed for forward firing by the pilot. Coupled with the RFC's relentless offensive strategy, the tactical superiority the Germans had enjoyed became more tenuous.

Regardless, the Albatros was still the same airplane and in the hands of aggressive pilots could go toe-to-toe with the new British machines and survive, even when outnumbered. In an undated event (likely April 1917) somewhat reminiscent of Werner Voss's mortal last combat, Lothar von Richthofen recalled an incident when he and his brother Manfred were attacked by five RFC airplanes of unidentified make and model (although possibly F.E.2s):

> Suddenly my brother and I saw five Englishmen who were coming down on us from a great height… At the moment they did not venture to come too close to us, but, rather, they remained above us and took practice shots. Then one became somewhat bolder and pounced on me. A quick turn and I sat behind him. The hunter became the prey.

The Englishman tried to save himself by flying west. Through continuous zigzag flying he did not offer me a sure target. Then he ceased his defensive movements. The observer appeared to me to be wounded. The Englishman already "stunk," a flying expression for the ribbon of smoke from a punctured fuel or oil tank. I was just ready to give the Englishman a final burst when my guns jammed. Deeply sorry, I let him go and turned away. In the course of the battle I had strayed many kilometers from our Front. Suddenly a frightful thought came to me: Where are the other four Englishmen and where is my brother? Then I saw a ghastly scene! The four Englishmen and my brother were turning circles around each other in a wild battle. I was fearful for Manfred. I had a gun jam and could no longer shoot. But he must have help! After all, my brother had continuously distracted the four Englishmen, who would have long since cut me off. Now it was my turn to help. I got right in the middle of the combatants. The four Englishmen, who had previously had one opponent, suddenly left us and flew home, even though they were double our number. They could not have known that my guns were jammed as well. As my brother said [figuratively] afterwards, he had given up on both our lives.

As a further effort to combat if not arrest Allied strategic air superiority, in June the Luftstreitkräfte organized Jastas 4, 6, 10, and 11 into Jagdgeschwader Nr I, a single cohesive unit "appointed for the purpose of fighting for and securing aerial superiority in crucial combat sectors," with Richthofen appointed as its first Kommandeur. According to JG1 Adjutant Karl Bodenschatz, on the evening of July 2 Richthofen assembled the four Staffelführers to discuss increasing enemy pressures endured by German ground troops:

[Richthofen's appraisal was] not pleasant to hear. The enemy's breakthrough attempts are being repeated again and again with a tenacity never yet experienced, and each new attack is more brutal and more bitter than the one before. The troops who have to endure these insane pushes are suffering terribly under a heavy barrage that never ends. And if, by some miracle, a break in the fire does occur, then infantry-support planes come roaring over right above the trenches and dugouts. And high above the infantry-support planes, whole clusters of bombing squadrons swing into the hinterland.

Jasta 4 pilot Leutnant Kurt Wüsthoff stands before his Albatros D.III(OAW), painted in Jasta 4 identifying black wound stripe. The various reflections of the high-gloss fuselage reveal the dents and wrinkles the birch skin accumulated over time. Note the axle fairing and round OAW valve access covers on the wheels.

Richthofen established direct telephonic communications with the front so that the Geschwader could be informed immediately of the presence of incoming British airplanes, and he implemented an attack hierarchy in lockstep with strategic considerations for support of the ground forces: (1) destruction of infantry-support planes; (2) destruction of the single-seater fighters; (3) destruction of the bombing squadrons.

Yet the improved British machines that arrived in increasing numbers rendered the April success an already distant memory as clashes with fighters increased throughout the summer. Casualties had also culled some of the Luftstreitkräfte's finest Albatros pilots, leaving a large summer void. Lothar von Richthofen was wounded on May 13 and would not return until September 24. Karl Schaefer was shot down and KiA June 5. Karl Allmenröder was shot down and KiA June 27. Manfred von Richthofen was wounded by a glancing shot to the head on July 6 that grounded him for weeks (although he had been flying an Albatros D.V, not D.III), after which he attained only two more victories flying an Albatros before being ordered away on recuperative leave. And Kurt Wolff was wounded on July 11 and would not return until September 11, only to be KiA four days later. These men were the pinnacle of Luftstreitkräfte aces and their absences were sorely felt throughout the summer.

The Luftstreitkräfte soldiered on, as did the Albatros D.IIIs, serving well into 1918 alongside Fokker's troubled Dr.I triplane and his far more successful design, the Fokker D.VII. As Greg VanWyngarden writes in Osprey's *Albatros Aces of World War I: Part 2*, the final front-line inventory of August 31, 1918 included 52 Albatros D.IIIs. By then the Albatros D production runs were over. The performance stagnation of their various D models and inability to impress Idflieg with new designs led to large D.VII production contracts for Fokker. Yet Albatros would be subcontracted to assist, producing the Fokker D.VII(Alb) and D.VII(OAW). With its larger production facilities, Albatros's contribution eclipsed that of Fokker, with Johannisthal and Schneidemühl manufacturing 2,200 D.VIIs compared with Fokker's 1,000.

CONCLUSION

Overall, the entire Albatros D.III line – D.III, D.III(OAW), and D.III(Oef) – was a success, especially during spring 1917 when German pilots flew their new Albatros against enemy airplane types "left over" from 1916. And although Albatros's sesquiplane design for their D-type fighter was troubled with structural failure, ultimately this problem was overcome well enough for German pilots still to enjoy marked success with the type.

Yet the positive regard held for the Albatros waned in 1917 as summer settled in and first the new Albatros D.V and then D.III(OAW) had arrived. Although fine airplanes in their own right, regardless of the D.V's continued lower-wing structural problems that the stronger-built D.III(OAW) avoided, better British machines arriving in increasing numbers eroded Germany's tactical aerial superiority and fostered a slow yet steady discontent with their front-line fighter. Since the previous autumn, new Albatros models had arrived every few months – the D.I in September 1916, the D.II in October 1916, the D.III in late December 1916/early January 1917, the D.V in May 1917, and the D.III(OAW) during the summer – yet anticipated performance increases

Albatros D.V prototype at Johannisthal, 1917. Unusually, the wooden fuselage – which has been redesigned from a slab-sided to fully ovoid cross-section, with lowered cockpit sides ostensibly to ease entry and egress – has been painted in five-color irregular polygon camouflage to match the wings. The vertical edge of the rudder soon gave way to a fully curved trailing edge, and the new headrest – disliked by pilots and often removed in-field – would soon be removed altogether from factory production. Unfortunately, despite this machine's good looks, the lower-wing structural problem that plagued the D.III carried over into this new design.

never arrived with these new models, while the performance of new British machines had increased markedly within the same period.

In Manfred von Richthofen's eyes, what had been gold in March and April had become slag by July. Writing about the Albatros D.III that summer, he noted: "A primary requirement of a fighter aircraft is that at higher altitudes in the sharpest turns, often 360 degrees at full throttle, the machine does not lose height. To gain altitude would be ideal. This is not the case with the Albatros D.III, its chief drawback."

It is unclear whether his opinion of the D.III's chief drawback was that it could not maintain altitude in a full-throttle steep turn or that it could not climb in a steep turn, or both. Regarding other aspects of the D.III's performance, he noted:

The ailerons must have a large effect with small movements, that is be very sensitive. The British have double ailerons. The Albatros D.III ailerons are not quite enough.

The Albatros D.III has a good rudder.

Visibility above, below, and to the sides must be impeccable. Albatros D.III good; Alb. D.II particularly poor below.

Richthofen's view on the new Albatros D.V was even worse. He wrote, "The DV is [so] outdated and so ridiculously inferior [to] the English single-seaters," and expressed frustration that for almost a year Germany had produced no better machines than "this lousy Albatros and [production has] stopped at Albatros D.III, with which I have already fought in the autumn of last year… So long as Albatros has no vigorous competition, we will sit in our D.III (V)." Indeed they would, for the next several months.

Austrian experiences and opinions were quite different. From the onset the D.III(Oef) was a fine machine that was well received. Built more robustly than the German D.III, it suffered no structural shortcomings, and with its bigger engine it enjoyed a higher airspeed as well. An ostentatious difference between the German and Austrian Albatros lineage was that while newly introduced German variants retained the same overall performance, new Austrian variants employed more powerful engines and structural redesign that provided continued performance improvements. By 1918, the 253-series Albatros D.III(Oef) employed a 225Ps engine that turned a spinner-less propeller in front of an aerodynamically redesigned fuselage. The result was "unquestionably the most maneuverable and safest fighter at the Front. It has the pilots' complete trust. Because of its excellent handling and performance, it is preferred over every other fighter."

Oeffag's production culminated with the D.III; they did not produce a D.V or D.Va model, as would Albatros. Postwar the D.III(Oef) was used by the Austrian Volkswehr in the Carinthian War, as well as by the Polish Air Force against Soviet Russia. In 1935 Oeffag was sold to Wiener-Nuestädter Flugzeugfabrik, which during World War II produced Messerschmitt Bf 109s. Heavily damaged as a result of Allied strategic bombing raids, the remaining production facilities were destroyed after the war by the occupying Soviet Army.

BIBLIOGRAPHY

Books

Connors, J. F., *Albatros Fighters in Action* (Squadron/Signal Publications, 1981)

Franks, N., *Jagdstaffel Boelcke* (Grub Street, 2004)

Gardner, B., *WW1 Aircraft Propellers, Volume Three* (self-published, 2008)

Grosz, P. M., *Fokker Fighters D.I–D.IV* (Windsock Classics of WW1 Aviation 2, Albatross Publications, 1999)

Grosz, P. M., *Albatros D.I/D.II* (Windsock Datafile 100, Albatross Publications, 2003)

Grosz, P. M., Haddow, G., and Schiemer, P., *Austro-Hungarian Army Aircraft of World War One* (Flying Machine Press, 1993)

Guttman, J., *The Origin of the Fighter Aircraft* (Westholme Publishing, 2009)

Guttman, J., *Pusher Aces of World War 1* (Osprey Publishing, 2009)

Hawker, T. M., *Hawker VC* (Mitre Press, 1965)

Höfling, R., *Albatros D-II: Germany's Legendary World War I Fighter* (Schiffer Books, 2002)

Kilduff, P., *The Red Baron* (Doubleday, 1969)

Kilduff, P., *Red Baron: The Life and Death of an Ace* (David & Charles Ltd, 2007)

Leaman, P., *Fokker Aircraft of World War One* (Crowood Press Ltd, 2001)

Lewis, G. H., *Wings Over the Somme 1916–1918* (William Kimber & Co Ltd, 1976)

McCudden, J., *Flying Fury: Five Years in the Royal Flying Corps* (Greenhill, 2000)

Mikesh, R. C., *Albatros D.Va, German Fighter of World War I* (Smithsonian Institution Press, 1980)

Miller, J. F., *Manfred von Richthofen: The Aircraft, Myths and Accomplishments of "The Red Baron"* (Air Power Editions, 2009)

O'Connor, M., *Air Aces of the Austro-Hungarian Empire 1914–1918* (Flying Machine Press, 1986)

Revell, A., *British Single-Seater Fighter Squadrons on the Western Front in World War I* (Schiffer, 2006)

Steel, N. and Hart, P., *Tumult in the Clouds* (Coronet Books, 1997)

Tesař, P., *Albatros D.II & D.III Oeffag* (JaPo, 1998)

VanWyngarden, G., *Early German Aces of World War 1* (Osprey Publishing, 2006)

VanWyngarden, G., *Albatros Aces of World War 1, Part 2* (Osprey Publishing, 2007)

VanWyngarden, G., *Jagdstaffel 2 "Boelcke": Von Richthofen's Mentor* (Osprey Publishing, 2007)

Varriale, P., *Austro-Hungarian Albatros Aces of World War 1* (Osprey Publishing, 2012)

Williams, A. G. and Gustin, E., *Flying Guns of World War I* (Crowood Press Ltd, 2003)

Articles

Fant, D. V., "Many Battles and Many a Bold Adventure," *Over the Front*, Vol 5, No 1, Spring 1990, pp 35–52

Gray, B. J., "The Anatomy of an Aeroplane," *Cross & Cockade International*, Vol 20, No 1, 1989, pp 1–25

Miller, J. F., "Eight Minutes Near Bapaume," *Over the Front*, Vol 21, No 2, Summer 2006, pp 120–38

INDEX